Great Writers on the Art of Fiction

From Mark Twain to Joyce Carol Oates

Edited By James Daley

D0957704

DOVER PUBLICATIONS, INC.
Mineola, New York

Bibliographical Note

Great Writers on the Art of Fiction is a new work, first published by Dover Publications, Inc., in 2007.

N.B. Page iii is an extension of the copyright page.

International Standard Book Number: 0-486-45128-3

Manufactured in the United States of America
Dover Publications, Inc., 31 East 2nd Street, Mineola, N.Y. 11501

Acknowledgments

"The Simple Art of Murder" from *The Simple Art of Murder* by Raymond Chandler. Copyright © 1950 by Raymond Chandler, © renewed 1978 by Helga Greene. Reprinted by permission of Houghton Mifflin Company. All rights reserved.

"To a Young Writer" from *On Teaching and Writing Fiction* by Wallace Stegner (Penguin, 2002). Copyright © 1959 by Wallace Stegner. Reprinted by permission of Don Congdon Associates, Inc.

"Words into Fiction" from *The Eye of the Story* by Eudora Welty, copyright © 1978 by Eudora Welty. Used by permission of Random House, Inc.

"On Writing" from *Fires* by Raymond Carver. Reprinted by permission of International Creative Management, Inc. Copyright © 1981 by Raymond Carver.

"How to Write with Style" from *Palm Sunday* by Kurt Vonnegut, copyright © 1981 by Kurt Vonnegut. Used by permission of Dell Publishing, a division of Random House, Inc.

"Nobody to Nobody" from *Negotiating with the Dead* by Margaret Atwood. Copyright © by O. W. Toad, Ltd. Reprinted with the permission of Cambridge University Press.

"Getting Started" by John Irving, reprinted from *Publishers Weekly*, February 2006. Copyright © Reed Business Information, a division of Reed Elsevier, Inc. All rights reserved.

"Running and Writing" from *The Faith of a Writer* by Joyce Carol Oates. Copyright © 2003 by The Ontario Review, Inc. Reprinted by permission of HarperCollins Publishers.

Introduction

By way of an introduction let's pretend, for a moment, that you are an aspiring writer, venturing into your local bookstore in search of a volume or two with which to enhance your expertise in the literary arts. You might suspect at first glance across the shelves marked WRITING, that there exists a plethora of valuable instruction books from which to choose. After all, with some fifty or sixty titles (if it is a small shop) staring you in the face, you *should* be able to simply pluck a few from the group and go on home to embark upon the practice of your craft. This is—you must agree—an altogether reasonable assumption.

The problem arises when you begin to inspect the authors of these books (for how else are you to judge which ones are worth your hard-earned money?) and quickly realize that, for the most part, you've neither heard of, nor read, a solitary one of them. At first, you chalk this up to some lack of your own knowledge, pull down a few of the more promising titles, and bring them over to the shelves marked FICTION. There you attempt to locate the great works their authors surely must have penned to qualify for teaching you how to "Write a Great Novel" or "Perfect Your Prose." Imagine your surprise, however, when you find nary a novel under their authorship. Or, if you do find one, it is definitely *not* the kind of novel you would ever desire to read, let alone want to write.

Clearly, this will not do. It is your aim to be a writer, so you want to read a book on writing by an author who has actually written something good—and preferably something that you yourself have read and admired. Of course, you may find a few works that come close to fulfilling this wish: a bit of criticism by an author you discovered in college, or a memoir by the writer of some guilty pleasure beach-read. You may even find an essay collection by a bona fide "master" that contains, at most, one or two chapters of usable advice and inspiration. In the end, even these examples are scarce, and the majority unsatisfying. You are then left with the dilemma of Coleridge's ancient mariner: "Water, water everywhere, nor any drop to drink." So many books on writing, yet none that will help you to write. It was as a direct response to this dilemma that the present anthology was conceived and created, so that you might open its pages to find useful and interesting essays on the art and craft of writing, by writers whose work you know and enjoy. In setting about the task of compiling this collection, it becomes clear almost immediately that the vast majority of writers commonly referred to as "great" have written absolutely nothing on the techniques of their craft. Furthermore (as previously noted) the vast majority of writers who have written on the subject would never, even in the most esoteric of circles, be referred to as "great." Luckily, however, this is more a matter of appearance than a fact, and persistent digging has led to the present volume.

The pieces included in the following pages do not, it should be emphasized, represent a complete "how to" guide to writing fiction. Although they do offer a good deal of practical and specific advice on the craft, they will not—individually or as a whole—launch the reader from the level of a beginning scribbler to that of a seasoned author. Reading this book with such an expectation would inevitably lead to disappointment. Instead, the writings that follow include a wide and diverse range of advice, critique, analysis, and philosophy. Each one is the meditation of a singular writer at a singular moment in time. Some will reference others directly, while some will contradict each other outright. In one essay you will find technical advice couched in a paragraph of analysis, and in another you will find analysis hidden in a paragraph of autobiography. It is quite likely that, within the same piece, you will find suggestions of great value side by side with advice that is of no worth to you at all. To put it simply: these essays are personal reflections on the purpose and practice of an art form, and as such, you should pick and choose what appeals to you in accordance with your own artistic inclinations.

In conclusion, read this book in the same way as you might converse with an old friend: do not look to be lectured, but rather seek to learn from these writers' mistakes, to heed their warnings, find enlightenment in their philosophies, and most importantly, to be inspired by the stories and ideas of those who have fought so well the battle of words for which you have here turned to arm yourself.

—JAMES DALEY

Contents

Edgar Allan Poe (1809–49)

"The Philosophy of Composition"

Known primarily for his poetry and short stories, Edgar Allan Poe's influence on literature cannot be overstated. His masterful short mystery, *Murders at the Rue Morgue*, gave rise to the entire genre of detective fiction, while his iconic poem, *The Raven*, is still at the apex of literary horror and suspense. His work has influenced a great diversity of writers: Poets such as W. H. Auden, Charles Baudelaire, and Walt Whitman, as well as fiction writers like Franz Kafka, William Faulkner, and Fyodor Dostoyevsky—have all spoken of Poe's powerful impact on their work.

In the essay that follows, Poe contends that good writing is not achieved by "ecstatic intuition," as some writers would have their readers believe, but through careful planning and consideration, executed with purposeful intention. To illustrate this point, Poe provides a step-by-step dissection of his own writing process during the composition of *The Raven*, explaining how he moved towards completion "with the precision and rigid consequence of a mathematical problem."

Charles Dickens, in a note now lying before me, alluding to an examination I once made of the mechanism of *Barnaby Rudge*, says: "By the way, are you aware that Godwin wrote his *Caleb Williams* backward? He first involved his hero in a web of difficulties, forming the second volume, and then, for the first, cast about him for some mode of accounting for what had been done."

I cannot think this the precise mode of procedure on the part of Godwin, and indeed what he himself acknowledges is not altogether in accordance with Mr. Dickens's idea; but the author of *Caleb Williams* was too good an artist not to perceive the advantage derivable from at least a somewhat similar process.

Nothing is more clear than that every plot, worth the name, must be elaborated to its *dénouement* before anything be attempted with the pen. It is only with the *dénouement* constantly in view that we can give a plot its indispensable air of consequence, or causation, by making the incidents, and especially the tone at all points, tend to the development of the intention.

There is a radical error, I think, in the usual mode of constructing a story. Either history affords a thesis, or one is suggested by an incident of the day, or, at best, the author sets himself to work in the combination of striking events to form merely the basis of his narrative, designing, generally, to fill in with description, dialogue, or authorial comment, whatever crevices of fact or action may, from page to page, render themselves apparent.

I prefer commencing with the consideration of an effect. Keeping originality always in view,—for he is false to himself who ventures to dispense with so obvious and so easily attainable a source of interest,—I say to myself, in the first place: "Of the innumerable effects, or impressions, of which the heart, the intellect, or (more generally) the soul is susceptible, what one shall I, on the present occasion, select?" Having chosen a novel, first, and secondly a vivid effect, I consider whether it can be best wrought by incident or tone,—whether by ordinary incidents and peculiar tone, or the converse, or by peculiarity both of incident and tone; afterward looking about me, or rather within, for such combinations of event, or tone, as shall best aid me in the construction of the effect.

I have often thought how interesting a magazine paper might be written by any author who would, that is to say, who could, detail, step by step, the processes by which any one of his compositions attained its ultimate point of completion. Why such a paper has never been given to the world I am much at a loss to say, but perhaps the authorial vanity has had more to do with the omission than any one other cause. Most writers, poets in especial, prefer having it understood that they compose by a species of fine frenzy, an ecstatic intuition, and would positively shudder at letting the public take a peep behind the scenes at the

elaborate and vacillating crudities of thought; at the true purposes seized only at the last moment; at the innumerable
glimpses of idea that arrived not at the maturity of full view; at
the full matured fancies discarded in despair as unmanageable;
at the cautious selections and rejections; at the painful erasures
and interpolations,—in a word, at the wheels and pinions, the
tackle for scene-shifting, the step-ladders and demon-traps, the
cock's feathers, the red paint and the black patches which, in
ninety-nine cases out of the hundred, constitute the properties
of the literary *histrio*.

I am aware, on the other hand, that the case is by no means
common in which an author is at all in condition to retrace the
steps by which his conclusions have been attained. In general,
suggestions, having arisen pell-mell, are pursued and forgotten
in a similar manner.

For my own part, I have neither sympathy with the repugnance alluded to, nor, at any time, the least difficulty in recall-
ing to mind the progressive steps of any of my compositions;
and, since the interest of an analysis, or reconstruction, such as
I have considered a desideratum, is quite independent of any
real or fancied interest in the thing analyzed, it will not be
regarded as a breach of decorum on my part to show the *modus
operandi* by which some one of my own works was put together.
I select *The Raven* as most generally known. It is my design to
render it manifest that no one point in its composition is refer-
able either to accident or intuition, that the work proceeded,
step by step, to its completion with the precision and rigid consequence of a mathematical problem.

Let us dismiss, as irrelevant to the poem *per se*, the circumstance, or say the necessity, which, in the first place, gave rise to
the intention of composing a poem that should suit at once the
popular and the critical taste.

We commence, then, with this intention.

The initial consideration was that of extent. If any literary
work is too long to be read at one sitting, we must be content to
dispense with the immensely important effect derivable from
unity of impression; for, if two sittings be required, the affairs of
the world interfere, and everything like totality is at once

destroyed. But since, *ceteris paribus*, no poet can afford to dispense with anything that may advance his design, it but remains to be seen whether there is, in extent, any advantage to counterbalance the loss of unity which attends it. Here I say no, at once. What we term a long poem is, in fact, merely a succession of brief ones; that is to say, of brief poetical effects. It is needless to demonstrate that a poem is such, only inasmuch as it intensely excites, by elevating, the soul; and all intense excitements are, through a physical necessity, brief. For this reason, at least one half of the *Paradise Lost* is essentially prose, a succession of poetical excitements interspersed, inevitably, with corresponding depressions, the whole being deprived, through the extremeness of its length, of the vastly important artistic element, totality, or unity, of effect.

It appears evident, then, that there is a distinct limit, as regards length, to all works of literary art—the limit of a single sitting—and that, although in certain classes of prose composition, such as *Robinson Crusoe* (demanding no unity), this limit may be advantageously overpassed, it can never properly be overpassed in a poem. Within this limit, the extent of a poem may be made to bear mathematical relation to its merit; in other words, to the excitement or elevation; again, in other words, to the degree of the true poetical effect which it is capable of inducing; for it is clear that the brevity must be in direct ratio of the intensity of the intended effect:—this, with one proviso, that a certain degree of duration is absolutely requisite for the production of any effect at all.

Holding in view these considerations, as well as that degree of excitement which I deemed not above the popular, while not below the critical, taste, I reached at once what I conceived the proper length for my intended poem, a length of about one hundred lines. It is, in fact, a hundred and eight.

My next thought concerned the choice of an impression, or effect, to be conveyed; and here I may as well observe that, throughout the construction, I kept steadily in view the design of rendering the work universally appreciable. I should be carried too far out of my immediate topic were I to demonstrate a point upon which I have repeatedly insisted, and which, with the poetical, stands not in the slightest need of demonstration—the point, I mean, that beauty is the sole legitimate province of the poem. A few words, however, in elucidation of my real meaning, which some of my friends have evinced a disposition to misrepresent. That pleasure which is at once the most intense, the most elevating, and the most pure, is, I believe, found in the contemplation of the beautiful. When, indeed, men speak of beauty, they mean, precisely, not a quality, as is supposed, but an effect; they refer, in short, just to that intense and pure elevation of soul, not of intellect or of heart, upon which I have commented, and which is experienced in consequence of contemplating "the beautiful." Now I designate beauty as the province of the poem, merely because it is an obvious rule of art that effects should be made to spring from direct causes, that objects should be attained through means best adapted for their attainment, no one as yet having been weak enough to deny that the peculiar elevation alluded to is most readily attained in the poem. Now the object, truth, or the satisfaction of the intellect, and the object, passion, or the excitement of the heart, are, although attainable to a certain extent in poetry, far more readily attainable in prose. Truth, in fact, demands a precision, and passion a homeliness (the truly passionate will comprehend me), which are absolutely antagonistic to that beauty which, I maintain, is the excitement, or pleasurable elevation, of the soul. It by no means follows from anything here said, that passion, or even truth, may not be introduced, and even profitably introduced, into a poem, for they may serve in elucidation, or aid the general effect, as do discords in music, by contrast; but the true artist will always contrive, first, to tone them into proper subservience to the predominant aim, and, secondly, to enveil them, as far as possible, in that beauty which is the atmosphere and the essence of the poem.

Regarding, then, beauty as my province, my next question referred to the tone of its highest manifestation, and all experience has shown that this tone is one of sadness. Beauty of whatever kind, in its supreme development, invariably excites the sensitive soul to tears. Melancholy is thus the most legitimate of all the poetical tones.

The length, the province, and the tone, being thus determined, I betook myself to ordinary induction, with the view of obtaining some artistic piquancy which might serve me as a keynote in the construction of the poem, some pivot upon which the whole structure might turn. In carefully thinking over all the usual artistic effects, or, more properly, points, in the theatrical sense, I did not fail to perceive immediately that no one had been so universally employed as that of the refrain. The universality of its employment sufficed to assure me of its intrinsic value, and spared me the necessity of submitting it to analysis. I considered it, however, with regard to its susceptibility of improvement, and soon saw it to be in a primitive condition. As commonly used, the refrain, or burden, not only is limited to lyric verse, but depends for its impression upon the force of monotone, both in sound and thought. The pleasure is deduced solely from the sense of identity—of repetition. I resolved to diversify, and so heighten, the effect, by adhering, in general, to the monotone of sound, while I continually varied that of thought: that is to say, I determined to produce continuously novel effects, by the variation of the application of the refrain, the refrain itself remaining, for the most part, unvaried.

These points being settled, I next bethought me of the nature of my refrain. Since its application was to be repeatedly varied, it was clear that the refrain itself must be brief, for there would have been an insurmountable difficulty in frequent variations of application in any sentence of length. In proportion to the brevity of the sentence, would, of course, be the facility of the variation. This led me at once to a single word as the best refrain.

The question now arose as to the character of the word. Having made up my mind to a refrain, the division of the poem into stanzas was, of course, a corollary, the refrain forming the close to each stanza. That such a close, to have force, must be sonorous and susceptible of protracted emphasis admitted no doubt; and these considerations inevitably led me to the long "o" as the most sonorous vowel, in connection with "r" as the most producible consonant.

The sound of the refrain being thus determined, it became necessary to select a word embodying this sound, and at the same time in the fullest possible keeping with that melancholy which I had predetermined as the tone of the poem. In such a search it would have been absolutely impossible to overlook the word "Nevermore." In fact, it was the very first which presented itself.

The next desideratum was a pretext for the continuous use of the one word "Nevermore." In observing the difficulty which I at once found in inventing a sufficiently plausible reason for its continuous repetition, I did not fail to perceive that this difficulty arose solely from the pre-assumption that the word was to be so continuously or monotonously spoken by a human being; I did not fail to perceive, in short, that the difficulty lay in the reconciliation of this monotony with the exercise of reason on the part of the creature repeating the word. Here, then, immediately arose the idea of a non-reasoning creature capable of speech; and, very naturally, a parrot, in the first instance, suggested itself, but was superseded forthwith by a Raven, as equally capable of speech, and infinitely more in keeping with the intended tone.

I had now gone so far as the conception of a Raven, the bird of ill omen, monotonously repeating the one word, "Nevermore," at the conclusion of each stanza, in a poem of melancholy tone, and in length about one hundred lines. Now, never losing sight of the object, supremeness, or perfection, at all points, I asked myself: "Of all melancholy topics, what, according to the universal understanding of mankind, is the most melancholy?" "Death" was the obvious reply. "And when," I said, "is this most melancholy of topics most poetical?" From what I have already explained at some length, the answer here, also, is obvious: "When it most closely allies itself to beauty: the death, then of a beautiful woman is, unquestionably, the most poetical topic in the world; and equally is it beyond doubt that the lips best suited for such topic are those of a bereaved lover."

I had now to combine the two ideas, of a lover lamenting his deceased mistress and a Raven continuously repeating the word "Nevermore." I had to combine these, bearing in mind my design of varying, at every turn, the application of the word repeated; but the only intelligible mode of such combination is that of imagining the Raven employing the word in answer to the queries of the lover. And here it was that I saw at once the opportunity afforded for the effect on which I had been depending; that is to say, the effect of the variation of application. I saw that I could make the first query propounded by the lover the first query to which the Raven should reply "Nevermore," that I could make this first query a commonplace one; the second less so, the third still less, and so on, until at length the lover, startled from his original nonchalance by the melancholy character of the word itself, by its frequent repetition, and by a consideration of the ominous reputation of the fowl that uttered it, is at length excited to superstition, and wildly propounds queries of a far different character,—queries whose solution he has passionately at heart,—propounds them half in superstition and half in that species of despair which delights in self-torture; propounds them not altogether because he believes in the prophetic or demoniac character of the bird (which, reason assures him, is merely repeating a lesson learned by rote), but because he experiences a frenzied pleasure in so modelling his questions as to receive from the expected "Nevermore" the most delicious because the most intolerable of sorrow. Perceiving the opportunity thus afforded me, or, more strictly, thus forced upon me in the progress of the construction, I first established in mind the climax, or concluding query—that query to which "Nevermore" should be in the last place an answer; that query in reply to which this word "Nevermore" should involve the utmost conceivable amount of sorrow and despair.

Here, then, the poem may be said to have its beginning—at the end, where all works of art should begin; for it was here, at this point of my preconsiderations, that I first put pen to paper in the composition of the stanza:

"Prophet," said I, "thing of evil! prophet still, if bird or devil!
By that heaven that bends above us, by that God we both adore,
Tell this soul with sorrow laden if, within the distant Aidenn,
It shall clasp a sainted maiden whom the angels name Lenore,
Clasp a rare and radiant maiden whom the angels name Lenore."
                    Quoth the Raven, "Nevermore."

I composed this stanza, at this point, first that, by establishing the climax, I might the better vary and graduate, as regards seriousness and importance, the preceding queries of the lover; and, secondly, that I might definitely settle the rhythm, the metre, and the length and general arrangement of the stanzas, as well as graduate the stanzas which were to precede, so that none of them might surpass this in rhythmical effect. Had I been able, in the subsequent composition, to construct more vigorous stanzas, I should, without scruple, have purposely enfeebled them, so as not to interfere with the climacteric effect.

And here I may as well say a few words of the versification. My first object, as usual, was originality. The extent to which this has been neglected in versification is one of the most unaccountable things in the world. Admitting that there is little possibility of variety in mere rhythm, it is still clear that the possible varieties of metre and stanza are absolutely infinite; and yet, for centuries, no man, in verse, has ever done, or ever seemed to think of doing, an original thing. The fact is, that originality, unless in minds of very unusual force, is by no means a matter, as some suppose, of impulse or intuition. In general, to be found, it must be elaborately sought, and although a positive merit of the highest class, demands in its attainment less of invention than negation.

Of course, I pretend to no originality in either the rhythm or metre of *The Raven*. The former is trochaic; the latter is octameter acatalectic, alternating with heptameter catalectic repeated in the refrain of the fifth verse, and terminating with tetrameter catalectic. Less pedantically, the feet employed throughout (trochees) consist of a long syllable followed by a short: the first line of the stanza consists of eight of these feet; the second of seven and a half (in effect two thirds); the third of eight; the fourth of seven and a half; the fifth the same; the sixth three and a half. Now, each of these lines, taken individually, has been employed before, and what originality *The Raven* has, is in their combination into stanza; nothing even remotely approaching this combination has ever been attempted. The effect of this originality of combination is aided by other unusual and some altogether novel effects, arising from an extension of the application of the principles of rhyme and alliteration.

The next point to be considered was the mode of bringing together the lover and the Raven, and the first branch of this consideration was the locale. For this the most natural suggestion might seem to be a forest or the fields, but it has always appeared to me that a close circumscription of space is absolutely necessary to the effect of insulated incident: it has the force of a frame to a picture. It has an indisputable moral power in keeping concentrated the attention, and, of course, must not be confounded with mere unity of place.

I determined, then, to place the lover in his chamber,—in a chamber rendered sacred to him by memories of her who had frequented it. The room is represented as richly furnished; this, in mere pursuance of the ideas I have already explained on the subject of beauty as the sole true poetical thesis.

The locale being thus determined, I had now to introduce the bird, and the thought of introducing him through the window was inevitable. The idea of making the lover suppose, in the first instance, that the flapping of the wings of the bird against the shutter is a "tapping" at the door originated in a wish to increase, by prolonging, the reader's curiosity, and in a desire to admit the incidental effect arising from the lover's throwing open the door, finding all dark, and thence adopting the half-fancy that it was the spirit of his mistress that knocked.

I made the night tempestuous, first, to account for the Raven's seeking admission, and, secondly, for the effect of contrast with the physical serenity within the chamber.

I made the bird alight on the bust of Pallas, also for the effect of contrast between the marble and the plumage,—it being understood that the bust was absolutely suggested by the bird; the bust of Pallas being chosen, first, as most in keeping with the scholarship of the lover, and, secondly, for the sonorousness of the word "Pallas" itself.

About the middle of the poem, also, I have availed myself of the force of contrast, with a view of deepening the ultimate impression. For example, an air of the fantastic, approaching as nearly to the ludicrous as was admissible, is given to the Raven's entrance. He comes in "with many a flirt and flutter."

Not the *least obeisance made he;* not a moment stopped or stayed he,
But with mien of lord or lady, perched above my chamber door.

In the two stanzas which follow, the design is more obviously carried out:

Then this ebony bird beguiling my sad fancy into smiling,
By the *grave and stern decorum of the countenance it wore,*
"Though thy *crest be shorn and shaven,* thou," I said, "art sure no
        craven,
Ghastly grim and ancient Raven wandering from the nightly shore;
Tell me what thy lordly name is on the Night's Plutonian shore?"
                                    Quoth the Raven, "Nevermore."

Much I marvelled *this ungainly fowl* to hear discourse so plainly,
Though its answer little meaning, little relevancy bore;
For we cannot help agreeing that no living human being
Ever yet was blest with seeing bird above his chamber door—
Bird or beast upon the sculptured bust above his chamber door,
                            With such name as, "Nevermore."

The effect of the *dénouement* being thus provided for, I immediately drop the fantastic for a tone of the most profound seriousness, this tone commencing in the stanza directly following the one last quoted, with the line,

But the Raven, sitting lonely on that placid bust, spoke only, etc.

From this epoch the lover no longer jests, no longer sees anything even of the fantastic in the Raven's demeanor. He speaks of him as a "grim, ungainly, ghastly, gaunt, and ominous bird of yore," and feels the "fiery eyes" burning into his "bosom's core." This revolution of thought, or fancy, on the lover's part is intended to induce a similar one on the part of the reader—to bring the mind into a proper frame for the *dénouement* which is now brought about as rapidly and as directly as possible.

With the *dénouement* proper—with the Raven's reply, "Nevermore," to the lover's final demand if he shall meet his mistress in another world, the poem, in its obvious phase, that of a single narrative, may be said to have its completion. So far, everything is within the limits of the accountable, of the real. A Raven, having learned by rote the single word, "Nevermore," and having escaped from the custody of its owner, is driven at midnight, through the violence of a storm, to seek admission at a window from which a light still gleams,—the chamber-window of a student, occupied half in poring over a volume, half in dreaming over a beloved mistress deceased. The casement being thrown open at the fluttering of a bird's wings, the bird itself perches on the most convenient seat out of the immediate reach of the student, who, amused by the incident and the oddity of the visitor's demeanor, demands of it, in jest and without looking for a reply, its name. The Raven, addressed, answers with its customary word, "Nevermore," a word which finds immediate echo in the melancholy heart of the student, who, giving utterance aloud to certain thoughts suggested by the occasion, is again startled by the fowl's repetition of "Nevermore." The student now guesses the state of the case, but is impelled, as I have before explained, by the human thirst for self-torture, and in part by superstition, to propound such queries to the bird as will bring him, the lover, the most of the luxury of sorrow, through the anticipated answer, "Nevermore." With the indulgence, to the extreme, of this self-torture, the narration, in what I have termed its first or obvious phase, has a natural termination, and so far there has been no overstepping of the limits of the real.

But in subjects so handled, however skilfully, or with however vivid an array of incident, there is always a certain hardness or nakedness, which repels the artistical eye. Two things are invariably required: first, some amount of complexity, or more properly, adaptation; and, secondly, some amount of suggestiveness, some undercurrent, however indefinite, of meaning. It is this latter, in especial, which imparts to a work of art so much of that richness (to borrow from colloquy a forcible term) which we are too fond of confounding with the ideal. It is the excess of the suggested meaning, it is the rendering this the upper- instead of the under-current of the theme, which turns into prose (and that of the very flattest kind) the so-called poetry of the so-called transcendentalists.

Holding these opinions, I added the two concluding stanzas of the poem, their suggestiveness being thus made to pervade all the narrative which has preceded them. The under-current of meaning is rendered first apparent in the lines,

"Take thy beak from out *my heart,* and take thy form from off my
   door;"
                                            Quoth the Raven, "Nevermore!"

It will be observed that the words, "from out my heart," involve the first metaphorical expression in the poem. They, with the answer, "Nevermore," dispose the mind to seek a moral in all that has been previously narrated. The reader begins now to regard the Raven as emblematical, but it is not until the very last line of the very last stanza that the intention of making him emblematical of mournful and never-ending remembrance is permitted distinctly to be seen:

And the Raven, never flitting, still is sitting, still is sitting
On the pallid bust of Pallas just above my chamber door;
And his eyes have all the seeming of a demon's that is dreaming,
And the lamplight o'er him streaming throws his shadow on the
   floor;
And my soul *from out that shadow* that lies floating on the floor
                                            Shall be lifted—nevermore.

                                                        (1846)

HENRY JAMES (1843–1916)

"THE ART OF FICTION"

One of America's most prolific writers, Henry James published twenty novels, over 100 stories, twelve plays, and countless essays over the course of his life. However, James is perhaps best remembered for his novellas, of which *The Turn of the Screw* and *Daisy Miller* are by far the most celebrated. Modeling himself on the likes of Charles Dickens and Nathaniel Hawthorne, Henry James is a force in all the modern American literature that succeeded him, particularly the work of Edith Wharton, Ernest Hemingway, and F. Scott Fitzgerald.

In *The Art of Fiction*, James offers an expansive analysis of the novel form that is at once critical, instructive, philosophical, and quite practical. Using the same distinct voice and characteristic prose that lent his fiction such renown, the essay is one of his greatest contributions—both to literary scholarship and the craft of fiction writing.

I should not have affixed so comprehensive a title to these few remarks, necessarily wanting in any completeness upon a subject the full consideration of which would carry us far, did I not seem to discover a pretext for my temerity in the interesting pamphlet lately published under this name by Mr. Walter Besant. Mr. Besant's lecture at the Royal Institution—the original form of his pamphlet—appears to indicate that many persons are interested in the art of fiction, and are not indifferent to such remarks, as those who practise it may attempt to make about it. I am therefore anxious not to lose the benefit of this favourable association, and to edge in a few words under cover of the attention which Mr. Besant is sure to have excited. There is something very encouraging in his having put into form certain of his ideas on the mystery of story-telling.

It is a proof of life and curiosity—curiosity on the part of the brotherhood of novelists as well as on the part of their readers.

Only a short time ago it might have been supposed that the
English novel was not what the French call *discutable*. It had no
air of having a theory, a conviction, a consciousness of itself
behind it—of being the expression of an artistic faith, the result
of choice and comparison. I do not say it was necessarily the
worse for that: it would take much more courage than I possess
to intimate that the form of the novel as Dickens and Thackeray
(for instance) saw it had any taint of incompleteness. It was,
however, *naïf* (if I may help myself out with another French
word); and evidently if it be destined to suffer in any way for
having lost its *naïveté* it has now an idea of making sure of the
corresponding advantages. During the period I have alluded to
there was a comfortable, good-humoured feeling abroad that a
novel is a novel, as a pudding is a pudding, and that our only
business with it could be to swallow it. But within a year or two,
for some reason or other, there have been signs of returning ani-
mation—the era of discussion would appear to have been to a
certain extent opened. Art lives upon discussion, upon experiment, upon curiosity, upon variety of attempt, upon the
exchange of views and the comparison of standpoints; and there
is a presumption that those times when no one has anything particular to say about it, and has no reason to give for practice or
preference, though they may be times of honour, are not times
of development—are times, possibly even, a little of dulness.
The successful application of any art is a delightful spectacle,
but the theory too is interesting; and though there is a great deal
of the latter without the former I suspect there has never been
a genuine success that has not had a latent core of conviction.
Discussion, suggestion, formulation, these things are fertilizing
when they are frank and sincere. Mr. Besant has set an excellent
example in saying what he thinks, for his part, about the way in
which fiction should be written, as well as about the way in
which it should be published; for his view of the "art," carried on
into an appendix, covers that too. Other labourers in the same
field will doubtless take up the argument, they will give it the
light of their experience, and the effect will surely be to make
our interest in the novel a little more what it had for some time
threatened to fail to be—a serious, active, inquiring interest,

under protection of which this delightful study may, in moments of confidence, venture to say a little more what it thinks of itself. It must take itself seriously for the public to take it so. The old superstition about fiction being "wicked" has doubtless died out in England; but the spirit of it lingers in a certain oblique regard directed toward any story which does not more or less admit that it is only a joke. Even the most jocular novel feels in some degree the weight of the proscription that was formerly directed against literary levity: the jocularity does not always succeed in passing for orthodoxy. It is still expected, though perhaps people are ashamed to say it, that a production which is after all only a "make-believe" (for what else is a "story"?) shall be in some degree apologetic—shall renounce the pretension of attempting really to represent life. This, of course, any sensible, wide-awake story declines to do, for it quickly perceives that the tolerance granted to it on such a condition is only an attempt to stifle it disguised in the form of generosity. The old evangelical hostility to the novel, which was as explicit as it was narrow, and which regarded it as little less favourable to our immortal part than a stage-play, was in reality far less insulting. The only reason for the existence of a novel is that it does attempt to represent life. When it relinquishes this attempt, the same attempt that we see on the canvas of the painter, it will have arrived at a very strange pass. It is not expected of the picture that it will make itself humble in order to be forgiven; and the analogy between the art of the painter and the art of the novelist is, so far as I am able to see, complete. Their inspiration is the same, their process (allowing for the different quality of the vehicle) is the same, their success is the same. They may learn from each other, they may explain and sustain each other. Their cause is the same, and the honour of one is the honour of another. The Mahometans think a picture an unholy thing, but it is a long time since any Christian did, and it is therefore the more odd that in the Christian mind the traces (dissimulated though they may be) of a suspicion of the sister art should linger to this day. The only effectual way to lay it to rest is to emphasize the analogy to which I just alluded—to insist on the fact that as the picture is reality, so the novel is history. That is the only general description (which does it justice) that we may give of the novel. But history also is allowed to represent life; it is not, any more than painting, expected to apologize. The subject-matter of fiction is stored up likewise in documents and records, and if it will not give itself away, as they say in California, it must speak with assurance, with the tone of the historian. Certain accomplished novelists have a habit of giving themselves away which must often bring tears to the eyes of people who take their fiction seriously. I was lately struck, in reading over many pages of Anthony Trollope, with his want of discretion in this particular. In a digression, a parenthesis or an aside, he concedes to the reader that he and this trusting friend are only "making believe." He admits that the events he narrates have not really happened, and that he can give his narrative any turn the reader may like best. Such a betrayal of a sacred office seems to me, I confess, a terrible crime; it is what I mean by the attitude of apology, and it shocks me every whit as much in Trollope as it would have shocked me in Gibbon or Macaulay. It implies that the novelist is less occupied in looking for the truth (the truth, of course I mean, that he assumes, the premises that we must grant him, whatever they may be) than the historian, and in doing so it deprives him at a stroke of all his standing-room. To represent and illustrate the past, the actions of men, is the task of either writer, and the only difference that I can see is, in proportion as he succeeds, to the honour of the novelist, consisting as it does in his having more difficulty in collecting his evidence, which is so far from being purely literary. It seems to me to give him a great character, the fact that he has at once so much in common with the philosopher and the painter; this double analogy is a magnificent heritage.

It is of all this evidently that Mr. Besant is full when he insists upon the fact that fiction is one of the *fine* arts, deserving in its turn of all the honours and emoluments that have hitherto been reserved for the successful profession of music, poetry, painting, architecture. It is impossible to insist too much on so important a truth, and the place that Mr. Besant demands for the work of the novelist may be represented, a trifle less abstractly, by saying that he demands not only that it shall be reputed artistic, but that it shall be reputed very artistic indeed. It is excellent that he should have struck this note, for his doing so indicates that there was need of it, that his proposition may be to many people a novelty. One rubs one's eyes at the thought; but the rest of Mr. Besant's essay confirms the revelation. I suspect in truth that it would be possible to confirm it still further, and that one would not be far wrong in saying that in addition to the people to whom it has never occurred that a novel ought to be artistic, there are a great many others who, if this principle were urged upon them, would be filled with an indefinable mistrust. They would find it difficult to explain their repugnance, but it would operate strongly to put them on their guard. "Art," in our Protestant communities, where so many things have got so strangely twisted about, is supposed in certain circles to have some vaguely injurious effect upon those who make it an important consideration, who let it weigh in the balance. It is assumed to be opposed in some mysterious manner to morality, to amusement, to instruction. When it is embodied in the work of the painter (the sculptor is another affair!) you know what it is: it stands there before you, in the honesty of pink and green and a gilt frame; you can see the worst of it at a glance, and you can be on your guard. But when it is introduced into literature it becomes more insidious—there is danger of its hurting you before you know it. Literature should be either instructive or amusing, and there is in many minds an impression that these artistic preoccupations, the search for form, contribute to neither end, interfere indeed with both. They are too frivolous to be edifying, and too serious to be diverting; and they are moreover priggish and paradoxical and superfluous. That, I think, represents the manner in which the latest thought of many people who read novels as an exercise in skipping would explain itself if it were to become articulate. They would argue, of course, that a novel ought to be "good," but they would interpret this term in a fashion of their own, which indeed would vary considerably from one critic to another. One would say that being good means representing virtuous and aspiring characters, placed in prominent positions; another would say that it depends on a "happy ending," on a distribution at the last of prizes, pensions, husbands,

wives, babies, millions, appended paragraphs, and cheerful
remarks. Another still would say that it means being full of incident and movement, so that we shall wish to jump ahead, to see
who was the mysterious stranger, and if the stolen will was ever
found, and shall not be distracted from this pleasure by any tire-
some analysis or "description." But they would all agree that the
"artistic" idea would spoil some of their fun. One would hold it
accountable for all the description, another would see it revealed
in the absence of sympathy. Its hostility to a happy ending would
be evident, and it might even in some cases render any ending
at all impossible. The "ending" of a novel is, for many persons,
like that of a good dinner, a course of dessert and ices, and the
artist in fiction is regarded as a sort of meddlesome doctor who
forbids agreeable aftertastes. It is therefore true that this
conception of Mr. Besant's of the novel as a superior form
encounters not only a negative but a positive indifference. It
matters little that as a work of art it should really be as little or
as much of its essence to supply happy endings, sympathetic
characters, and an objective tone, as if it were a work of mechan-
ics: the association of ideas, however incongruous, might easily
be too much for it if an eloquent voice were not sometimes
raised to call attention to the fact that it is at once as free and as
serious a branch of literature as any other.

Certainly this might sometimes be doubted in presence of the
enormous number of works of fiction that appeal to the credulity of our generation, for it might easily seem that there could be
no great character in a commodity so quickly and easily produced. It must be admitted that good novels are much compromised by bad ones, and that the field at large suffers discredit
from overcrowding. I think, however, that this injury is only
superficial, and that the superabundance of written fiction
proves nothing against the principle itself. It has been vulgar-
ized, like all other kinds of literature, like everything else to-day,
and it has proved more than some kinds accessible to vulgariza-
tion. But there is as much difference as there ever was between
a good novel and a bad one: the bad is swept with all the daubed
canvases and spoiled marble into some unvisited limbo, or infinite rubbish-yard beneath the back-windows of the world, and

the good subsists and emits its light and stimulates our desire for perfection. As I shall take the liberty of making but a single criticism of Mr. Besant, whose tone is so full of the love of his art, I may as well have done with it at once. He seems to me to mistake in attempting to say so definitely beforehand what sort of an affair the good novel will be. To indicate the danger of such an error as that has been the purpose of these few pages; to suggest that certain traditions on the subject, applied *a priori,* have already had much to answer for, and that the good health of an art which undertakes so immediately to reproduce life must demand that it be perfectly free. It lives upon exercise, and the very meaning of exercise is freedom. The only obligation to which in advance we may hold a novel, without incurring the accusation of being arbitrary, is that it be interesting. That general responsibility rests upon it, but it is the only one I can think of. The ways in which it is at liberty to accomplish this result (of interesting us) strike me as innumerable, and such as can only suffer from being marked out or fenced in by prescription. They are as various as the temperament of man, and they are successful in proportion as they reveal a particular mind, different from others. A novel is in its broadest definition a personal, a direct impression of life: that, to begin with, constitutes its value, which is greater or less according to the intensity of the impression. But there will be no intensity at all, and therefore no value, unless there is freedom to feel and say. The tracing of a line to be followed, of a tone to be taken, of a form to be filled out, is a limitation of that freedom and a suppression of the very thing that we are most curious about. The form, it seems to me, is to be appreciated after the fact: then the author's choice has been made, his standard has been indicated; then we can follow lines and directions and compare tones and resemblances. Then in a word we can enjoy one of the most charming of pleasures, we can estimate quality, we can apply the test of execution. The execution belongs to the author alone; it is what is most personal to him, and we measure him by that. The advantage, the luxury, as well as the torment and responsibility of the novelist, is that there is no limit to what he may attempt as an executant— no limit to his possible experiments, efforts, discoveries, successes. Here it is especially that he works, step by step, like his brother of the brush, of whom we may always say that he has painted his picture in a manner best known to himself. His manner is his secret, not necessarily a jealous one. He cannot disclose it as a general thing if he would; he would be at a loss to teach it to others. I say this with a due recollection of having insisted on the community of method of the artist who paints a picture and the artist who writes a novel. The painter *is* able to teach the rudiments of his practice, and it is possible, from the study of good work (granted the aptitude), both to learn how to paint and to learn how to write. Yet it remains true, without injury to the *rapprochement,* that the literary artist would be obliged to say to his pupil much more than the other, "Ah, well, you must do it as you can!" It is a question of degree, a matter of delicacy. If there are exact sciences, there are also exact arts, and the grammar of painting is so much more definite that it makes the difference.

I ought to add, however, that if Mr. Besant says at the beginning of his essay that the "laws of fiction may be laid down and taught with as much precision and exactness as the laws of harmony, perspective, and proportion," he mitigates what might appear to be an extravagance by applying his remark to "general" laws, and by expressing most of these rules in a manner with which it would certainly be unaccommodating to disagree. That the novelist must write from his experience, that his "characters must be real and such as might be met with in actual life"; that "a young lady brought up in a quiet country village should avoid descriptions of garrison life," and "a writer whose friends and personal experiences belong to the lower middle-class should carefully avoid introducing his characters into society"; that one should enter one's notes in a common-place book; that one's figures should be clear in outline; that making them clear by some trick of speech or of carriage is a bad method, and "describing them at length" is a worse one; that English Fiction should have a "conscious moral purpose"; that "it is almost impossible to estimate too highly the value of careful workmanship—that is, of style"; that "the most important point of all is the story," that "the story is everything": these are principles with most of which it is surely impossible not to sympathize. That remark about the lower middle-class writer and his knowing his place is perhaps rather chilling; but for the rest I should find it difficult to dissent from any one of these recommendations. At the same time, I should find it difficult positively to assent to them, with the exception, perhaps, of the injunction as to entering one's notes in a common-place book. They scarcely seem to me to have the quality that Mr. Besant attributes to the rules of the novelist— the "precision and exactness" of "the laws of harmony, perspective, and proportion." They are suggestive, they are even inspiring, but they are not exact, though they are doubtless as much so as the case admits of: which is a proof of that liberty of interpretation for which I just contended. For the value of these different injunctions—so beautiful and so vague—is wholly in the meaning one attaches to them. The characters, the situation, which strike one as real will be those that touch and interest one most, but the measure of reality is very difficult to fix. The reality of Don Quixote or of Mr. Micawber is a very delicate shade; it is a reality so coloured by the author's vision, that, vivid as it may be, one would hesitate to propose it as a model: one would expose one's self to some very embarrassing questions on the part of a pupil. It goes without saying that you will not write a good novel unless you possess the sense of reality; but it will be difficult to give you a recipe for calling that sense into being. Humanity is immense, and reality has a myriad forms; the most one can affirm is that some of the flowers of fiction have the odour of it, and others have not; as for telling you in advance how your nosegay should be composed, that is another affair. It is equally excellent and inconclusive to say that one must write from experience; to our suppositions aspirant such a declaration might savour of mockery. What kind of experience is intended, and where does it begin and end? Experience is never limited, and it is never complete; it is an immense sensibility, a kind of huge spider-web of the finest silken threads suspended in the chamber of consciousness, and catching every air-borne particle in its tissue. It is the very atmosphere of the mind; and when the mind is imaginative—much more when it happens to be that of a man of genius—it takes to itself the faintest hints of life, it converts the very pulses of the air into revelations. The young lady living in a village has only to be a damsel upon whom nothing is lost to make it quite unfair (as it seems to me) to declare to her that she shall have nothing to say about the military. Greater miracles have been seen than that, imagination assisting, she should speak the truth about some of these gentlemen. I remember an English novelist, a woman of genius, telling me that she was much commended for the impression she had managed to give in one of her tales of the nature and way of life of the French Protestant youth. She had been asked where she learned so much about this recondite being, she had been congratulated on her peculiar opportunities. These opportunities consisted in her having once, in Paris, as she ascended a staircase, passed an open door where, in the household of a *pasteur,* some of the young Protestants were seated at table round a finished meal. The glimpse made a picture; it lasted only a moment, but that moment was experience. She had got her direct personal impression, and she turned out her type. She knew what youth was, and what Protestantism; she also had the advantage of having seen what it was to be French, so that she converted these ideas into a concrete image and produced a reality. Above all, however, she was blessed with the faculty which when you give it an inch takes an ell, and which for the artist is a much greater source of strength than any accident of residence or of place in the social scale. The power to guess the unseen from the seen, to trace the implication of things, to judge the whole piece by the pattern, the condition of feeling life in general so completely that you are well on your way to knowing any particular corner of it—this cluster of gifts may almost be said to constitute experience, and they occur in country and in town, and in the most differing stages of education. If experience consists of impressions, it may be said that impressions *are* experience, just as (have we not seen it?) they are the very air we breathe. Therefore, if I should certainly say to a novice, "Write from experience and experience only," I should feel that this was rather a tantalizing monition if I were not careful immediately to add, "Try to be one of the people on whom nothing is lost!"

I am far from intending by this to minimize the importance of exactness—of truth of detail. One can speak best from one's own taste, and I may therefore venture to say that the air of reality (solidity of specification) seems to me to be the supreme virtue of a novel—the merit on which all its other merits (including that conscious moral purpose of which Mr. Besant speaks) helplessly and submissively depend. If it be not there they are all as nothing, and if these be there, they owe their effect to the success with which the author has produced the illusion of life. The cultivation of this success, the study of this exquisite process, form, to my taste, the beginning and the end of the art of the novelist. They are his inspiration, his despair, his reward, his torment, his delight. It is here in very truth that he competes with life; it is here that he competes with his brother the painter in *his* attempt to render the look of things, the look that conveys their meaning, to catch the colour, the relief, the expression, the surface, the substance of the human spectacle. It is in regard to this that Mr. Besant is well inspired when he bids him take notes. He cannot possibly take too many, he cannot possibly take enough. All life solicits him, and to "render" the simplest surface, to produce the most momentary illusion, is a very complicated business. His case would be easier, and the rule would be more exact, if Mr. Besant had been able to tell him what notes to take. But this, I fear, he can never learn in any manual; it is the business of his life. He has to take a great many in order to select a few, he has to work them up as he can, and even the guides and philosophers who might have most to say to him must leave him alone when it comes to the application of precepts, as we leave the painter in communion with his palette. That his characters "must be clear in outline," as Mr. Besant says—he feels that down to his boots; but how he shall make them so is a secret between his good angel and himself. It would be absurdly simple if he could be taught that a great deal of "description" would make them so, or that on the contrary the absence of description and the cultivation of dialogue, or the absence of dialogue and the multiplication of "incident," would rescue him from his difficulties. Nothing, for instance, is more possible than that he be of a turn of mind for which this odd, literal opposition of description and dialogue, incident and description, has little meaning and light. People often talk of these things as if they had a kind of internecine distinctness, instead of melting into each other at every breath, and being intimately associated parts of one general effort of expression. I cannot imagine composition existing in a series of blocks, nor conceive, in any novel worth discussing at all, of a passage of description that is not in its intention narrative, a passage of dialogue that is not in its intention descriptive, a touch of truth of any sort that does not partake of the nature of incident, or an incident that derives its interest from any other source than the general and only source of the success of a work of art—that of being illustrative. A novel is a living thing, all one and continuous, like any other organism, and in proportion as it lives will it be found, I think, that in each of the parts there is something of each of the other parts. The critic who over the close texture of a finished work shall pretend to trace a geography of items will mark some frontiers as artificial, I fear, as any that have been known to history. There is an old-fashioned distinction between the novel of character and the novel of incident which must have cost many a smile to the intending fabulist who was keen about his work. It appears to me as little to the point as the equally celebrated distinction between the novel and the romance—to answer as little to any reality. There are bad novels and good novels, as there are bad pictures and good pictures; but that is the only distinction in which I see any meaning, and I can as little imagine speaking of a novel of character as I can imagine speaking of a picture of character. When one says picture one says of character, when one says novel one says of incident, and the terms may be transposed at will. What is character but the determination of incident? What is incident but the illustration of character? What is either a picture or a novel that is *not* of character? What else do we seek in it and find in it? It is an incident for a woman to stand up with her hand resting on a table and look out at you in a certain way; or if it be not an incident I think it will be hard to say what it is. At the same time it is an expression of character. If you say you don't see it (character in *that—allons donc!*), this is exactly what the artist who has reasons of his own for thinking he *does* see it undertakes to show you.

When a young man makes up his mind that he has not faith enough after all to enter the church as he intended, that is an incident, though you may not hurry to the end of the chapter to see whether perhaps he doesn't change once more. I do not say that these are extraordinary or startling incidents. I do not pretend to estimate the degree of interest proceeding from them, for this will depend upon the skill of the painter. It sounds almost puerile to say that some incidents are intrinsically much more important than others, and I need not take this precaution after having professed my sympathy for the major ones in remarking that the only classification of the novel that I can understand is into that which has life and that which has it not.

The novel and the romance, the novel of incident and that of character—these clumsy separations appear to me to have been made by critics and readers for their own convenience, and to help them out of some of their occasional queer predicaments, but to have little reality or interest for the producer, from whose point of view it is of course that we are attempting to consider the art of fiction. The case is the same with another shadowy category which Mr. Besant apparently is disposed to set up— that of the "modern English novel"; unless indeed it be that in this matter he has fallen into an accidental confusion of standpoints. It is not quite clear whether he intends the remarks in which he alludes to it to be didactic or historical. It is as difficult to suppose a person intending to write a modern English as to suppose him writing an ancient English novel: that is a label which begs the question. One writes the novel, one paints the picture, of one's language and of one's time, and calling it modern English will not, alas! make the difficult task any easier. No more, unfortunately, will calling this or that work of one's fellow-artist a romance—unless it be, of course, simply for the pleasantness of the thing, as for instance when Hawthorne gave this heading to his story of *Blithedale*. The French, who have brought the theory of fiction to remarkable completeness, have but one name for the novel, and have not attempted smaller things in it, that I can see, for that. I can think of no obligation to which the "romancer" would not be held equally with the novelist; the standard of execution is equally high for each. Of course it is of execution that we are talking—that being the only point of a novel that is open to contention. This is perhaps too often lost sight of, only to produce interminable confusions and cross-purposes. We must grant the artist his subject, his idea, his *donnée:* our criticism is applied only to what he makes of it. Naturally I do not mean that we are bound to like it or find it interesting: in case we do not our course is perfectly simple—to let it alone. We may believe that of a certain idea even the most sincere novelist can make nothing at all, and the event may perfectly justify our belief; but the failure will have been a failure to execute, and it is in the execution that the fatal weakness is recorded. If we pretend to respect the artist at all, we must allow him his freedom of choice, in the face, in particular cases, of innumerable presumptions that the choice will not fructify. Art derives a considerable part of its beneficial exercise from flying in the face of presumptions, and some of the most interesting experiments of which it is capable are hidden in the bosom of common things. Gustave Flaubert has written a story about the devotion of a servant-girl to a parrot, and the production, highly finished as it is, cannot on the whole be called a success. We are perfectly free to find it flat, but I think it might have been interesting; and I, for my part, am extremely glad he should have written it; it is a contribution to our knowledge of what can be done—or what cannot. Ivan Turgénieff has written a tale about a deaf and dumb serf and a lap-dog, and the thing is touching, loving, a little masterpiece. He struck the note of life where Gustave Flaubert missed it—he flew in the face of a presumption and achieved a victory.

Nothing, of course, will ever take the place of the good old fashion of "liking" a work of art or not liking it: the most improved criticism will not abolish that primitive, that ultimate test. I mention this to guard myself from the accusation of intimating that the idea, the subject, of a novel or a picture, does not matter. It matters, to my sense, in the highest degree, and if I might put up a prayer it would be that artists should select none but the richest. Some, as I have already hastened to admit, are much more remunerative than others, and it would be a world happily arranged in which persons intending to treat them should be exempt from confusions and mistakes. This fortunate condition will arrive only, I fear, on the same day that critics become purged from error. Meanwhile, I repeat, we do not judge the artist with fairness unless we say to him,

"Oh, I grant you your starting-point, because if I did not I should seem to prescribe to you, and heaven forbid I should take that responsibility. If I pretend to tell you what you must not take, you will call upon me to tell you then what you must take; in which case I shall be prettily caught. Moreover, it isn't till I have accepted your data that I can begin to measure you. I have the standard, the pitch; I have no right to tamper with your flute and then criticize your music. Of course I may not care for your idea at all; I may think it silly, or stale, or unclean; in which case I wash my hands of you altogether. I may content myself with believing that you will not have succeeded in being interesting, but I shall, of course, not attempt to demonstrate it, and you will be as indifferent to me as I am to you. I needn't remind you that there are all sorts of tastes: who can know it better? Some people, for excellent reasons, don't like to read about carpenters; others, for reasons even better, don't like to read about courtesans. Many object to Americans. Others (I believe they are mainly editors and publishers) won't look at Italians. Some readers don't like quiet subjects; others don't like bustling ones. Some enjoy a complete illusion, others the consciousness of large concessions. They choose their novels accordingly, and if they don't care about your idea they won't, *a fortiori*, care about your treatment."

So that it comes back very quickly, as I have said, to the liking: in spite of M. Zola, who reasons less powerfully than he represents, and who will not reconcile himself to this absoluteness of taste, thinking that there are certain things that people ought to like, and that they can be made to like. I am quite at a loss to imagine anything (at any rate in this matter of fiction) that people *ought* to like or to dislike. Selection will be sure to take care of itself, for it has a constant motive behind it. That motive is simply experience. As people feel life, so they will feel the art that is most closely related to it. This closeness of relation is what we should never forget in talking of the effort of the novel. Many people speak of it as a factitious, artificial form, a product of ingenuity, the business of which is to alter and arrange the things that surround us, to translate them into conventional, traditional moulds. This, however, is a view of the matter which carries us but a very short way, condemns the art to an eternal repetition of a few familiar *clichés*, cuts short its development, and leads us straight up to a dead wall. Catching the very note and trick, the strange irregular rhythm of life, that is the attempt whose strenuous force keeps Fiction upon her feet. In proportion as in what she offers us we see life *without* rearrangement do we feel that we are touching the truth; in proportion as we see it *with* rearrangement do we feel that we are being put off with a substitute, a compromise and convention. It is not uncommon to hear an extraordinary assurance of remark in regard to this matter of rearranging, which is often spoken of as if it were the last word of art. Mr. Besant seems to me in danger of falling into the great error with his rather unguarded talk about "selection." Art is essentially selection, but it is a selection whose main care is to be typical, to be inclusive. For many people art means rose-coloured window-panes, and selection means picking a bouquet for Mrs. Grundy. They will tell you glibly that artistic considerations have nothing to do with the disagreeable, with the ugly; they will rattle off shallow commonplaces about the province of art and the limits of art till you are moved to some wonder in return as to the province and the limits of ignorance. It appears to me that no one can ever have made a seriously artistic attempt without becoming conscious of an immense increase—a kind of revelation—of freedom. One perceives in that case—by the light of a heavenly ray—that the province of art is all life, all feeling, all observation, all vision. As Mr. Besant so justly intimates, it is all experience. That is a sufficient answer to those who maintain that it must not touch the sad things of life, who stick into its divine unconscious bosom little prohibitory inscriptions on the end of sticks, such as we see in public gardens—"It is forbidden to walk on the grass; it is forbidden to touch the flowers; it is not allowed to introduce dogs or to remain after dark; it is requested to keep to the right." The young aspirant in the line of fiction whom we continue to imagine will do nothing without taste, for in that case his freedom would be of little use to him; but the first advantage of his taste will be to reveal to him the absurdity of the little sticks and tickets. If he have taste, I must add, of course he will have ingenuity, and my disrespectful reference to that quality just now was not meant to imply that it is useless in fiction. But it is only a secondary aid; the first is a capacity for receiving straight impressions.

Mr. Besant has some remarks on the question of "the story" which I shall not attempt to criticize, though they seem to me to contain a singular ambiguity, because I do not think I understand them. I cannot see what is meant by talking as if there were a part of a novel which is the story and part of it which for mystical reasons is not—unless indeed the distinction be made in a sense in which it is difficult to suppose that any one should attempt to convey anything. "The story," if it represents anything, represents the subject, the idea, the *donnée* of the novel; and there is surely no "school"—Mr. Besant speaks of a school—which urges that a novel should be all treatment and no subject. There must assuredly be something to treat; every school is intimately conscious of that. This sense of the story being the idea, the starting-point, of the novel, is the only one that I see in which it can be spoken of as something different from its organic whole; and since in proportion as the work is successful the idea permeates and penetrates it, informs and animates it, so that every word and every punctuation-point contribute directly to the expression, in that proportion do we lose our sense of the story being a blade which may be drawn more or less out of its sheath. The story and the novel, the idea and the form, are the needle and thread, and I never heard of a guild of tailors who recommended the use of the thread without the needle, or the needle without the thread. Mr. Besant is not the only critic who may be observed to have spoken as if there were certain things in life which constitute stories, and certain others which do not. I find the same odd implication in an entertaining article in the *Pall Mall Gazette*, devoted, as it happens, to Mr. Besant's lecture. "The story is the thing!" says this graceful writer, as if with a tone of opposition to some other idea. I should think it was, as every painter who, as the time for "sending in" his picture looms in the distance, finds himself still in quest of a subject—as every belated artist not fixed about his theme will heartily agree. There are some subjects which speak to us and others which do not, but he would be a clever man who should undertake to give a rule—an *index expurgatorius*—

by which the story and the no-story should be known apart. It is impossible (to me at least) to imagine any such rule which shall not be altogether arbitrary. The writer in the *Pall Mall* opposes the delightful (as I suppose) novel of *Margot la Balafrée* to certain tales in which "Bostonian nymphs" appear to have "rejected English dukes for psychological reasons." I am not acquainted with the romance just designated, and can scarcely forgive the *Pall Mall* critic for not mentioning the name of the author, but the title appears to refer to a lady who may have received a scar in some heroic adventure. I am inconsolable at not being acquainted with this episode, but am utterly at a loss to see why it is a story when the rejection (or acceptance) of a duke is not, and why a reason, psychological or other, is not a subject when a cicatrix is. They are all particles of the multitudinous life with which the novel deals, and surely no dogma which pretends to make it lawful to touch the one and unlawful to touch the other will stand for a moment on its feet. It is the special picture that must stand or fall, according as it seem to possess truth or to lack it. Mr. Besant does not, to my sense, light up the subject by intimating that a story must, under penalty of not being a story, consist of "adventures." Why of adventures more than of green spectacles? He mentions a category of impossible things, and among them he places "fiction without adventure." Why without adventure, more than without matrimony, or celibacy, or parturition, or cholera, or hydropathy, or Jansenism? This seems to me to bring the novel back to the hapless little *rôle* of being an artificial, ingenious thing—bring it down from its large, free character of an immense and exquisite correspondence with life. And what *is* adventure, when it comes to that, and by what sign is the listening pupil to recognize it? It is an adventure—an immense one—for me to write this little article; and for a Bostonian nymph to reject an English duke is an adventure only less stirring, I should say, than for an English duke to be rejected by a Bostonian nymph. I see dramas within dramas in that, and innumerable points of view. A psychological reason is, to my imagination, an object adorably pictorial; to catch the tint of its complexion—I feel as if that idea might inspire one to Titianesque efforts. There are few things more exciting to me, in short, than a psychological reason, and yet, I protest, the novel seems to me the most magnificent form of art. I have just been reading, at the same time, the delightful story of *Treasure Island,* by Mr. Robert Louis Stevenson and, in a manner less consecutive, the last tale from M. Edmond de Goncourt, which is entitled *Chérie.* One of these works treats of murders, mysteries, islands of dreadful renown, hair-breadth escapes, miraculous coincidences and buried doubloons. The other treats of a little French girl who lived in a fine house in Paris, and died of wounded sensibility because no one would marry her. I call *Treasure Island* delightful, because it appears to me to have succeeded wonderfully in what it attempts; and I venture to bestow no epithet upon *Chérie,* which strikes me as having failed deplorably in what it attempts—that is in tracing the development of the moral consciousness of a child. But one of these productions strikes me as exactly as much of a novel as the other, and as having a "story" quite as much. The moral consciousness of a child is as much a part of life as the islands of the Spanish Main, and the one sort of geography seems to me to have those "surprises" of which Mr. Besant speaks quite as much as the other. For myself (since it comes back in the last resort, as I say, to the preference of the individual), the picture of the child's experience has the advantage that I can at successive steps (an immense luxury, near to the "sensual pleasure" of which Mr. Besant's critic in the *Pall Mall* speaks) say Yes or No, as it may be, to what the artist puts before me. I have been a child in fact, but I have been on a quest for a buried treasure only in supposition, and it is a simple accident that with M. de Goncourt I should have for the most part to say No. With George Eliot, when she painted that country with a far other intelligence, I always said Yes.

The most interesting part of Mr. Besant's lecture is unfortunately the briefest passage—his very cursory allusion to the "conscious moral purpose" of the novel. Here again it is not very clear whether he be recording a fact or laying down a principle; it is a great pity that in the latter case he should not have developed his idea. This branch of the subject is of immense importance, and Mr. Besant's few words point to considerations of the

widest reach, not to be lightly disposed of. He will have treated
the art of fiction but superficially who is not prepared to go every
inch of the way that these considerations will carry him. It is for
this reason that at the beginning of these remarks I was careful
to notify the reader that my reflections on so large a theme have
no pretension to be exhaustive. Like Mr. Besant, I have left the
question of the morality of the novel till the last, and at the last
I find I have used up my space. It is a question surrounded with
difficulties, as witness the very first that meets us, in the form of
a definite question, on the threshold. Vagueness, in such a discussion, is fatal, and what is the meaning of your morality and
your conscious moral purpose? Will you not define your terms
and explain how (a novel being a picture) a picture can be either
moral or immoral? You wish to paint a moral picture or carve a
moral statue: will you not tell us how you would set about it? We
are discussing the Art of Fiction; questions of art are questions
(in the widest sense) of execution; questions of morality are
quite another affair, and will you not let us see how it is that you
find it so easy to mix them up? These things are so clear to Mr.
Besant that he has deduced from them a law which he sees
embodied in English Fiction, and which is "a truly admirable
thing and a great cause for congratulation." It is a great cause for
congratulation indeed when such thorny problems become as
smooth as silk. I may add that in so far as Mr. Besant perceives
that in point of fact English Fiction has addressed itself prepon-
derantly to these delicate questions he will appear to many
people to have made a vain discovery. They will have been positively struck, on the contrary, with the moral timidity of the usual
English novelist; with his (or with her) aversion to face the difficulties with which on every side the treatment of reality bristles.
He is apt to be extremely shy (whereas the picture that Mr.
Besant draws is a picture of boldness), and the sign of his work,
for the most part, is a cautious silence on certain subjects. In the
English novel (by which of course I mean the American as well),
more than in any other, there is a traditional difference between
that which people know and that which they agree to admit that
they know, that which they see and that which they speak of, that
which they feel to be a part of life and that which they allow to

enter into literature. There is the great difference, in short, between what they talk of in conversation and what they talk of in print. The essence of moral energy is to survey the whole field, and I should directly reverse Mr. Besant's remark and say not that the English novel has a purpose, but that it has a diffidence. To what degree a purpose in a work of art is a source of corruption I shall not attempt to inquire; the one that seems to me least dangerous is the purpose of making a perfect work. As for our novel, I may say lastly on this score that as we find it in England to-day it strikes me as addressed in a large degree to "young people," and that this in itself constitutes a presumption that it will be rather shy. There are certain things which it is generally agreed not to discuss, not even to mention, before young people. That is very well, but the absence of discussion is not a symptom of the moral passion. The purpose of the English novel—"a truly admirable thing, and a great cause for congratulation"—strikes me therefore as rather negative.

There is one point at which the moral sense and the artistic sense lie very near together; that is in the light of the very obvious truth that the deepest quality of a work of art will always be the quality of the mind of the producer. In proportion as that intelligence is fine will the novel, the picture, the statue partake of the substance of beauty and truth. To be constituted of such elements is, to my vision, to have purpose enough. No good novel will ever proceed from a superficial mind; that seems to me an axiom which, for the artist in fiction, will cover all needful moral ground: if the youthful aspirant take it to heart it will illuminate for him many of the mysteries of "purpose." There are many other useful things that might be said to him, but I have come to the end of my article, and can only touch them as I pass. The critic in the *Pall Mall Gazette*, whom I have already quoted, draws attention to the danger, in speaking of the art of fiction, of generalizing. The danger that he has in mind is rather, I imagine, that of particularizing, for there are some comprehensive remarks which, in addition to those embodied in Mr. Besant's suggestive lecture, might without fear of misleading him be addressed to the ingenuous student. I should remind him first of the magnificence of the form that is open to him, which offers to sight so few restrictions and such innumerable opportunities. The other arts, in comparison, appear confined and hampered; the various conditions under which they are exercised are so rigid and definite. But the only condition that I can think of attaching to the composition of the novel is, as I have already said, that it be sincere. This freedom is a splendid privilege, and the first lesson of the young novelist is to learn to be worthy of it.

"Enjoy it as it deserves [I should say to him]; take possession of it, explore it to its utmost extent, publish it, rejoice in it. All life belongs to you, and do not listen either to those who would shut you up into corners of it and tell you that it is only here and there that art inhabits, or to those who would persuade you that this heavenly messenger wings her way outside of life altogether, breathing a superfine air, and turning away her head from the truth of things. There is no impression of life, no manner of seeing it and feeling it, to which the plan of the novelist may not offer a place; you have only to remember that talents so dissimilar as those of Alexandre Dumas and Jane Austen, Charles Dickens and Gustave Flaubert have worked in this field with equal glory. Do not think too much about optimism and pessimism; try and catch the colour of life itself. In France to-day we see a prodigious effect (that of Emile Zola, to whose solid and serious work no explorer of the capacity of the novel can allude without respect), we see an extraordinary effort vitiated by a spirit of pessimism on a narrow basis. M. Zola is magnificent, but he strikes an English reader as ignorant; he has an air of working in the dark; if he had as much light as energy, his results would be of the highest value. As for the aberrations of a shallow optimism, the ground (of English fiction especially) is strewn with their brittle particles as with broken glass. If you must indulge in conclusions, let them have the taste of a wide knowledge. Remember that your first duty is to be as complete as possible—to make as perfect a work. Be generous and delicate and pursue the prize."

(1888)

JOSEPH CONRAD (1857–1924)

"CONRAD'S MANIFESTO"

Although Joseph Conrad ranks as one of the greatest English-language novelists, he did not actually learn the language until the age of twenty (while serving in the British merchant navy), or begin writing fiction until well into his thirties. Born Jósef Teodor Konrad Korzeniowski on December 3, 1857 in the Polish Ukraine, Conrad remained with the navy until the age of thirty-six, when he quit to become an author. His first novel, *Almayer's Folly*, was published in 1895, followed shortly thereafter by *An Outcast of the Islands*, *The Nigger of the 'Narcissus,'* and his most famous work, the novella *Heart of Darkness*. Originally printed in *Blackwood's Magazine* as a three-part series, *Heart of Darkness* was the inspiration for the 1979 film *Apocalypse Now*, and remains one of the most widely read and highly respected works of fiction in the English language.

The following essay is the preface to *The Nigger of the 'Narcissus,'* although it came to be known as *Conrad's Manifesto* when David R. Smith published it separately, along with a history and facsimile of the original manuscript, in *Conrad's Manifesto: Preface to a Career* (Philadelphia: Philip H. and A.S.W. Rosenbach Foundation, 1966). In this brief and passionate piece, Conrad expounds upon the nature of art, what literature must accomplish to become art, and how the writer should approach his craft to achieve this end.

A work that aspires, however humbly, to the condition of art should carry its justification in every line. And art itself may be defined as a single-minded attempt to render the highest kind of justice to the visible universe, by bringing to light the truth, manifold and one, underlying its every aspect. It is an attempt to find in its forms, in its colours, in its light, in its shadows, in the aspects of matter and in the facts of life, what of each is fundamental, what is enduring and essential—their one illuminating and convincing quality—the very truth of their existence. The artist, then, like the thinker or the scientist, seeks the truth and makes his appeal. Impressed by the aspect of the world the thinker plunges into ideas, the scientist into facts—whence, presently emerging, they make their appeal to those qualities of our being that fit us best for the hazardous enterprise of living. They speak authoritatively to our common sense, to our intelligence, to our desire of peace, or to our desire of unrest; not seldom to our prejudices, sometimes to our fears, often to our egoism—but always to our credulity. And their words are heard with reverence, for their concern is with weighty matters; with the cultivation of our minds and the proper care of our bodies; with the attainment of our ambitions; with the perfection of the means and the glorification of our precious aims.

It is otherwise with the artist.

Confronted by the same enigmatical spectacle the artist descends within himself, and in that lonely region of stress and strife, if he be deserving and fortunate, he finds the terms of his appeal. His appeal is made to our less obvious capacities; to that part of our nature which, because of the warlike conditions of existence, is necessarily kept out of sight within the more resisting and hard qualities—like the vulnerable body within a steel armour. His appeal is less loud, more profound, less distinct, more stirring—and sooner forgotten. Yet its effect endures for ever. The changing wisdom of successive generations discards ideas, questions facts, demolishes theories. But the artist appeals to that part of our being which is not dependent on wisdom; to that in us which is a gift and not an acquisition—and, therefore, more permanently enduring. He speaks to our capacity for delight and wonder, to the sense of mystery surrounding our lives; to our sense of pity, and beauty, and pain; to the latent feeling of fellowship with all creation; and to the subtle but invincible conviction of solidarity that knits together the loneliness of innumerable hearts: to that solidarity in dreams, in joy, in sorrow, in aspirations, in illusions, in hope, in fear, which binds men to each other, which binds together all humanity—the dead to the living, and the living to the unborn.

It is only some such train of thought, or rather of feeling, that can in a measure explain the aim of the attempt made in the tale which follows, to present an unrestful episode in the obscure lives of a few individuals out of all the disregarded multitude of the bewildered, the simple, and the voiceless. For, if there is any part of truth in the belief confessed above, it becomes evident that there is not a place of splendour or a dark corner of the earth that does not deserve, if only a passing glance of wonder and pity. The motive, then, may be held to justify the matter of the work; but this preface, which is simply an avowal of endeavour, cannot end here—for the avowal is not yet complete.

Fiction—if it at all aspires to be art—appeals to temperament. And in truth it must be, like painting, like music, like all art, the appeal of one temperament to all the other innumerable temperaments whose subtle and resistless power endows passing events with their true meaning, and creates the moral, the emotional atmosphere of the place and time. Such an appeal, to be effective, must be an impression conveyed through the senses; and, in fact, it cannot be made in any other way, because temperament, whether individual or collective, is not amenable to persuasion. All art, therefore, appeals primarily to the senses, and the artistic aim when expressing itself in written words must also make its appeal through the senses, if its high desire is to reach the secret spring of responsive emotions. It must strenuously aspire to the plasticity of sculpture, to the colour of painting, and to the magic suggestiveness of music—which is the art of arts. And it is only through complete, unswerving devotion to the perfect blending of form and substance; it is only through an unremitting, never-discouraged care for the shape and ring of sentences, that an approach can be made to plasticity, to colour; and the light of magic suggestiveness may be brought to play for an evanescent instant over the commonplace surface of words: of the old, old words, worn thin, defaced by ages of careless usage.

The sincere endeavour to accomplish that creative task, to go as far on that road as his strength will carry him, to go undeterred by faltering, weariness, or reproach, is the only valid justification for the worker in prose. And if his conscience is clear, his answer to those who, in the fulness of a wisdom which looks for immediate profit, demand specifically to be edified, consoled, amused; who demand to be promptly improved, or encouraged, or frightened, or shocked, or charmed, must run thus: My task which I am trying to achieve is, by the power of the written word, to make you hear, to make you feel—it is, before all, to make you *see!* That—and no more: and it is everything! If I succeed, you shall find there according to your deserts: encouragement, consolation, fear, charm—all you demand; and, perhaps, also that glimpse of truth for which you have forgotten to ask.

To snatch in a moment of courage, from the remorseless rush of time, a passing phase of life, is only the beginning of the task. The task approached in tenderness and faith is to hold up unquestioningly, without choice and without fear, the rescued fragment before all eyes and in the light of a sincere mood. It is to show its vibration, its colour, its form; and through its movement, its form, and its colour, reveal the substance of its truth—disclose its inspiring secret: the stress and passion within the core of each convincing moment. In a single-minded attempt of that kind, if one be deserving and fortunate, one may perchance attain to such clearness of sincerity that at last the presented vision of regret or pity, of terror or mirth, shall awaken in the hearts of the beholders that feeling of unavoidable solidarity; of the solidarity in mysterious origin, in toil, in joy, in hope, in uncertain fate—which binds men to each other and all mankind to the visible world.

It is evident that he who, rightly or wrongly, holds by the convictions expressed above cannot be faithful to any one of the temporary formulas of his craft. The enduring part of them—the truth which each only imperfectly veils—should abide with him as the most precious of his possessions, but they all: Realism, Romanticism, Naturalism; even the unofficial sentimentalism (which, like the poor, is exceedingly difficult to get rid of); all these gods must, after a short period of fellowship, abandon him—even on the very threshold of the temple—to the stammerings of his conscience and to the outspoken consciousness of the difficulties of his work. In that uneasy solitude the cry of Art for Art itself, loses the exciting ring of its apparent immorality. It sounds far off. It has ceased to be a cry, and is heard only as a whisper, often incomprehensible, but at times, and faintly, encouraging.

Sometimes, stretched at ease in the shade of a roadside tree, we watch the motions of a labourer in a distant field, and, after a time, begin to wonder languidly as to what the fellow may be at. We watch the movements of his body, the waving of his arms; we see him bend down, stand up, hesitate, begin again. It may add to the charm of an idle hour to be told the purpose of his exertions. If we know he is trying to lift a stone, to dig a ditch, to uproot a stump, we look with a more real interest at his efforts; we are disposed to condone the jar of his agitation upon the restfulness of the landscape; and even, if in a brotherly frame of mind, we may bring ourselves to forgive his failure. We understood his object, and, after all, the fellow has tried, and perhaps he had not the strength—and perhaps he had not the knowledge. We forgive, go on our way—and forget.

And so it is with the workman of art. Art is long and life is short, and success is very far off. And thus, doubtful of strength to travel so far, we talk a little about the aim—the aim of art, which, like life itself, is inspiring, difficult—obscured by mists. It is not in the clear logic of a triumphant conclusion; it is not in the unveiling of one of those heartless secrets which are called the Laws of Nature. It is not less great, but only more difficult!

To arrest, for the space of a breath, the hands busy about the work of the earth, and compel men entranced by the sight of distant goals to glance for a moment at the surrounding vision of form and colour, of sunshine and shadows; to make them pause for a look, for a sigh, for a smile—such is the aim, difficult and evanescent, and reserved only for a very few to achieve. But sometimes, by the deserving and the fortunate, even that task is accomplished. And when it is accomplished—behold! all the truth of life is there: a moment of vision, a sigh, a smile—and the return to an eternal rest.

(1897)

KATE CHOPIN (1851–1904)

"MY WRITING METHOD"

Although Kate Chopin (born Katherine O'Flaherty in 1851) was raised among the upper crust of St. Louis society, the writing for which she grew famous chronicled the life and culture of New Orleans—the home of her husband, Oscar Chopin. After first making a name for herself as a writer of "local color" in stories for magazines such as the *Atlantic Monthly, Criterion,* and *Vogue,* Chopin went on to write *The Awakening,* her first literary success. Although widely condemned at the time as vulgar for its bold exploration of female sexuality, *The Awakening* is now recognized as a work that was far ahead of its time and a true American masterpiece.

In this short essay, first written for the St. Louis *Post-Dispatch* in 1899, Chopin answers the multifaceted question, "'How, where, when, why, what do you write?'" Seeming to suppress the urge for sarcasm in every line, she dutifully responds to each of these inquiries, and in the process offers precious insight into how she herself approached her craft.

Eight or nine years ago I began to write stories—short stories which appeared in the magazines, and I forthwith began to suspect I had the writing habit. The public shared this impression, and called me an author. Since then, though I have written many short stories and a novel or two, I am forced to admit that I have not the writing habit. But it is hard to make people with the questioning habit believe this.

"How, where, when, why, what do you write?" are some of the questions that I remember. How do I write? On a lapboard with a block of paper, a stub pen, and a bottle of ink bought at the corner grocery, which keeps the best in town.

Where do I write? In a Morris chair beside the window, where I can see a few trees and a patch of sky, more or less blue.

When do I write? I am greatly tempted here to use slang and reply "any old time," but that would lend a tone of levity to this bit of confidence, whose seriousness I want to keep intact if possible. So I shall say I write in the morning, when not too strongly drawn to struggle with the intricacies of a pattern, and in the afternoon, if the temptation to try a new furniture polish on an old table leg is not too powerful to be denied; sometimes at night, though as I grow older I am more and more inclined to believe that night was made for sleep.

"Why do I write?" is a question which I have often asked myself and never very satisfactorily answered. Story-writing—at least with me—is the spontaneous expression of impressions gathered goodness knows where. To seek the source, the impulse of a story is like tearing a flower to pieces for wantonness.

What do I write? Well, not everything that comes into my head, but much of what I have written lies between the covers of my books.

There are stories that seem to write themselves, and others which positively refuse to be written—which no amount of coaxing can bring to anything. I do not believe any writer has ever made a "portrait" in fiction. A trick, a mannerism, a physical trait or mental characteristic go a very short way towards portraying the complete individual in real life who suggests the individual in the writer's imagination. The "material" of a writer is to the last degree uncertain, and I fear not marketable. I have been told stories which were looked upon as veritable gold mines by the generous narrators who placed them at my disposal. I have been taken to spots supposed to be alive with local color. I have been introduced to excruciating characters with frank permission to use them as I liked, but never, in any single instance, has such material been of the slightest service. I am completely at the mercy of unconscious selection. To such an extent is this true, that what is called the polishing up process has always proved disastrous to my work, and I avoid it, preferring the integrity of crudities to artificialities.

(1899)

JACK LONDON (1876–1916)

"ADVICE FOR ASPIRING WRITERS"

Jack London was born John Griffith Chaney in San Francisco on January 12, 1876. Essentially self-educated, London began writing at the age of twenty-one, when he was unable to find any other type of work after dropping out of the University of California at Berkeley. Although his first book, *The Son of the Wolf*, gained a wide audience, London wrote his greatest works in the succeeding decade with *The Call of the Wild* in 1903, *White Fang* in 1906, and his famous short story, *To Build a Fire*, in 1908. Over the course of his career, Jack London published fifty books of fiction and nonfiction, and became at the time the highest paid writer in the United States.

What follows are five separate writings by London. The first is an essay entitled "On the Writer's Philosophy of Life"—originally published in *The Editor* in 1899—which contains advice for the aspiring writer. The remaining four are letters, written in response to young writers' requests for guidance. In both the essay and the letters, London's suggestions are sometimes kind, sometimes stern, but always blunt. Most notable is his insistence that to be a great writer, one must invest considerable time and effort, that one must think of learning to write as serving an apprenticeship of many years—sometimes committing to "many a long month nineteen hours a day." He challenges young writers to work tirelessly at their craft if their aim is to achieve the level of success that he enjoyed. In his own words: "I plugged. Can you plug this way for 19 hours a day?"

The literary hack, the one who is satisfied to turn out "pot boilers" for the rest of his or her life, will save time and vexation by passing this article by. It contains no hints as to the disposing of manuscript, the vagaries of the blue-pencil, the filing of material, nor the innate perversity of adjectives and adverbs. Petrified "Pen-trotters," pass on! This is for the writer—no matter how much hack-work he is turning out just now—who cherishes ambitions and ideals, and yearns for the time when agricultural newspapers and home magazines no more may occupy the major portion of his visiting list.

How are you, dear sir, madam, or miss, to achieve distinction in the field you have chosen? Genius? Oh, but you are no genius. If you were you would not be reading these lines. Genius is irresistible; it casts aside all shackles and restraints; it cannot be held down. Genius is a *rara avis,* not to be found fluttering in every grove as are you and I. But then you are talented? Yes, in an embryonic sort of way. The biceps of Hercules was a puny affair when he rolled about in swaddling-clothes. So with you—your talent is undeveloped. If it had received proper nutrition and were well matured, you would not be wasting your time over this. And if you think your talent really has attained its years of discretion, stop right here. If you think it has not, then by what methods do you think it will?

By being original, you at once suggest; then add, *and by constantly strengthening that originality.* Very good. But the question is not merely being original—the veriest tyro knows that much—but now can you become original? How are you to cause the reading world to look eagerly for your work? to force the publishers to pant for it? You cannot expect to become original by following the blazed trail of another, by reflecting the radiations of some one else's originality. No one broke ground for Scott or Dickens, for Poe or Longfellow, for George Eliot or Mrs. Humphrey Ward, for Stevenson and Kipling, Anthony Hope, Stephen Crane, and many others of the lengthening list. Yet publishers and public have clamored for their ware. They conquered originality. And how? By not being silly weathercocks, turning to every breeze that flows. They, with the countless failures, started even in the race; the world with its traditions was their common heritage. But in one thing they differed from the failures; they drew straight from the source, rejecting the material which filtered through other hands. They had no use for the conclusions and the conceits of others. They must put the stamp of "self" upon their work—a trade mark of far greater value than copyright. So, from the world and its traditions—which is another term for knowledge and culture—

they drew at first hand, certain materials, which they builded into an individual philosophy of life.

Now this phrase, "a philosophy of life," will not permit of precise definition. In the first place it does not mean a philosophy on any one thing. It has no especial concern with any one of such questions as the past and future travail of the soul, the double and single standard of morals for the sexes, the economic independence of women, the possibility of acquired characters being inherited, spiritualism, reincarnation, temperance, etc. But it is concerned with all of them, in a way, and with all the other ruts and stumbling blocks which confront the man or woman who really lives. In short, it is an ordinary working philosophy of life.

Every permanently successful writer has possessed this philosophy. It was a view peculiarly his own. It was a yardstick by which he measured all things which came to his notice. By it he focused the characters he drew, the thoughts he uttered. Because of it his work was sane, normal, and fresh. It was something new, something the world wished to hear. It was his, and not a garbled mouthing of things the world had already heard.

But make no mistake. The possession of such a philosophy does not imply a yielding to the didactic impulse. Because one may have pronounced views on any question is no reason that he assault the public ear with a novel with a purpose, and for that matter, no reason that he should not. But it will be noticed, however, that this philosophy of the writer rarely manifests itself in a desire to sway the world to one side or the other of any problem. Some few great writers have been avowedly didactic, while some, like Robert Louis Stevenson, in a manner at once bold and delicate, have put themselves almost wholly into their work, and done so without once imparting the idea that they had something to teach.

And it must be understood that such a working philosophy enables the writer to put not only himself into his work, but to put that which is not himself but which is viewed and weighted by himself. Of none is this more true than of that triumvirate of intellectual giants—Shakespeare, Goethe, Balzac. Each was himself, and so much so, that there is no point of comparison.

Each had drawn from this store his own working philosophy. And by this individual standard they accomplished their work. At birth they must have been very similar to all infants; but somehow, from the world and its traditions, they acquired something which their fellows did not. And this was neither more nor less than *something to say.*

Now you, young writer, have you something to say, or do you merely think you have something to say? If you have, there is nothing to prevent your saying it. If you are capable of thinking thoughts which the world would like to hear, the very form of the thinking is the expression. If you think clearly, you will write clearly; if your thoughts are worthy, so will your writing be worthy. But if your expression is poor, it is because your thought is poor, if narrow, because you are narrow. If your ideas are confused and jumbled, how can you expect a lucid utterance? If your knowledge is sparse or unsystematized, how can your words be broad or logical? And without the strong central thread of a working philosophy, how can you make order out of chaos? how can your foresight and insight be clear? how can you have a quantitive and qualitative perception of the relative importance of every scrap of knowledge you possess? And without all this how can you possibly be yourself? how can you have something fresh for the jaded ear of the world?

The only way of gaining this philosophy is by seeking it, by drawing the materials which go to compose it from the knowledge and culture of the world. What do you know of the world beneath its bubbling surface? What can you know of the bubbles unless you comprehend the forces at work in the depths of the cauldron? Can an artist paint an "Ecce Homo" without having a conception of the Hebrew myths and history, and all the varied traits which form collectively the character of the Jew, his beliefs and ideals, his passions and his pleasures, his hopes and fears! Can a musician compose a "Ride of the Valkyries" and know nothing of the great Teutonic epics? So with you—you must study. You must come to read the face of life with understanding. To comprehend the characters and phases of any movement, you must know the spirit which moves to action individuals and peoples, which gives birth and momentum to great ideas, which hangs a John Brown or crucifies a Savior. You must have your hand on the inner pulse of things. And the sum of all this will be your working philosophy, by which, in turn, you will measure, weigh, and balance, and interpret to the world. It is this stamp of personality of individual view, which is known as individuality.

What do you know of history, biology, evolution, ethics, and the thousand and one branches of knowledge? "But," you object, "I fail to see how such things can aid me in the writing of a romance or a poem." Ah, but they will. They broaden your thought, lengthen out your vistas, drive back the bounds of the field in which you work. They give you your philosophy, which is like unto no other man's philosophy, force you to original thought.

"But the task is stupendous," you protest; "I have no time." Others have not been deterred by its immensity. The years of your life are at your own disposal. Certainly you cannot expect to master it all, but in the proportion you do master it, just so will your efficiency increase, just so will you command the attention of your fellows. Time! When you speak of its lack you mean lack of economy in its use. Have you really learned *how* to read? How many insipid short stories and novels do you read in the course of a year, endeavoring either to master the art of story-writing or of exercising your critical faculty? How many magazines do you read clear through from beginning to end? There's time for you, time you have been wasting with a fool's prodigality—time which can never come again. Learn to discriminate in the selection of your reading and learn to skim judiciously. You laugh at the doddering graybeard who reads the daily paper, advertisements and all. But is it less pathetic, the spectacle you present in trying to breast the tide of current fiction? But don't shun it. Read the best, and the best only. Don't finish a tale simply because you have commenced it. Remember that you are a writer, first, last and always. Remember that these are the mouthings of others, and if you read them exclusively, that you may garble them; you will have nothing else to write about. Time! If you cannot find time, rest assured that the world will not find time to listen to you.

(1899)

Glen Ellen, Calif.
Sept. 28, 1913

Dear friend Jess Dorman:

In reply to yours of Sept. 25, 1913. Assuming, to quote you, that you "have in mind an original virile story," that you are "capable of writing it," I should say, if you wrote it, at the rate of 1000 words a day, and sold it as an unknown at an unknown's price (which would be at least 2¢ for such a virile, original, well-written story), I leave the arithmetic to you.

If you are earning more than $20 a day, then leave it alone; if you are earning less than $20 a day, write the story.

Please know that I am answering your letter according to the very rigid stipulations that you laid down to me. Since, as you say, you know my career, you must know that I worked many a long month nineteen hours a day, without sleep, and sold a great deal of my stuff at 75¢ per 100 words for stories that were not original, that were not virile, that were not well written.

I plugged. Can you plug this way for 19 hours a day?

You say you cannot so plug. If you say truth, well, far be in from me to advise you to tackle such a game.

If you think you can jump in right now, without any apprenticeship, and lay bricks as well as a four, five, or six years' apprenticed brick-layer; if you think you can jump in on the floor and nail on shoes on ten horses as well as a man who has served a three, four, or five years' apprenticeship at shoeing horses on the floor; if you think you can jump in and nail laths, or spread plaster, or do concrete work, without previous experience, better or as well as the men who have served their three, four, and five years of apprenticeship;—in short, if you think that a vastly better-paid trade than that, namely, the writing-game, can be achieved in your first short story not yet written, or long story not yet written, why go ahead my boy and jump to it, and I'll pat you on the back—pat you on the back! the world will crush you in for the great genius that you are if you can do such a thing. In the mean-time have a little patience and learn the trade.

If you know my career, you know that I am a brass-tack man. And I have given you brass tacks right here. If you can beat all the rest of us, without serving your apprenticeship, go to it. Far be it from us to advise you.

Sincerely yours,
Jack London

Oakland, Calif.
Oct. 26, 1914

Dear Max Feckler:

In reply to yours of recent date undated, and returning herewith your Manuscript. First of all, let me tell you that as a psychologist and as one who has been through the mill, I enjoyed your story for its psychology and point of view. Honestly and frankly, I did not enjoy it for its literary charm or value. In the first place, it has little literary value and practically no literary charm. Merely because you have got something to say that may be of interest to others does not free you from making all due effort to express that something in the best possible medium and form. Medium and form you have utterly neglected.

Anent the foregoing paragraph, what is to be expected of any lad of twenty, without practice, in knowledge of medium and form? Heavens on earth, boy, it would take you five years to serve your apprenticeship and become a skilled blacksmith. Will you dare to say that you have spent, not five years, but as much as five months of unimpeachable, unremitting toil in trying to learn the artisan's tools of a professional writer who can sell his stuff to the magazines and receive hard cash for same? Of course you cannot; you have not done it. And yet, you should be able to reason on the face of it that the only explanation for the fact that successful writers receive such large fortunes, is because very few who desire to write become successful writers. If it takes five years work to become a skilled blacksmith, how many years of work intensified into nineteen hours a day, so that one year counts for five—how many years of such work, studying medium and form, art and artisanship, do you think a man, with native talent and something to say, required in order to reach a place in the world of letters where he received a thousand dollars cash iron money per week?

I think you get the drift of the point I am trying to make. If a fellow harnesses himself to a star of $1000 week, he has to work proportionately harder than if he harnesses himself to a little glowworm of $20.00 a week. The only reason there are more successful blacksmiths in the world than successful writers, is that it is much easier, and requires far less hard work to become a successful blacksmith than does it to become a successful writer.

It cannot be possible that you, at twenty, should have done the work at writing that would merit you success at writing. You have not begun your apprenticeship yet. The proof of it is the fact that you dared to write this manuscript, "A Journal of One Who Is to Die." Had you made any sort of study of what is published in the magazines you would have found that your short story was of the sort that never was published in the magazines. If you are going to write for success and money, you must deliver to the market marketable goods. Your short story is not marketable goods, and had you taken half a dozen evenings off and gone into a free reading room and read all the stories published in the current magazines, you would have learned in advance that your short story was not marketable goods.

Dear lad, I'm talking to you straight from the shoulder. Remember one very important thing: Your ennui of twenty, is your ennui of twenty. You will have various other and complicated ennuis before you die. I tell you this, who have been through the ennui of sixteen as well as the ennui of twenty; and the boredom, and the blaséness, and utter wretchedness of the ennui of twenty-five, and of thirty. And I yet live, am growing fat, am very happy, and laugh a large portion of my waking hours. You see, the disease has progressed so much further with me than with you that I, as a battle-scarred survivor of the disease, look upon your symptoms as merely the preliminary adolescent symptoms. Again, let me tell you that I know them, that I had them, and just as I had much worse afterward of the same sort, so much worse is in store for you. In the meantime, if you want to succeed at a well-paid game, prepare yourself to do the work.

There's only one way to make a beginning, and that is to begin; and begin with hard work, and patience, prepared for all the disappointments that were Martin Eden's before he succeeded—which were mine before I succeeded—because I merely appended to my fictional character, Martin Eden, my own experiences in the writing game.

Any time you are out here in California, I should be glad to have you come to visit me on the ranch. I can meet you to the last limit of brass tacks, and hammer some facts of life into you that possibly so far have escaped your own experience.

Sincerely yours,
Jack London

Glen Ellen, Calif.
Dec. 11, 1914

My dear Miss Andersen:

In my opinion, three positive things are necessary for success as a writer. First a study and knowledge of literature as it is commercially produced today.

Second, a knowledge of life, and

Third, a working philosophy of life.

Negatively, I would suggest that the best preparation for authorship is a stern refusal to accept blindly the canons of literary art as laid down by teachers of high school English and teachers of university English and composition.

The average author is lucky, I mean the average successful author is lucky, if he makes twelve hundred to two thousand dollars a year.

Many successful authors earn in various ways from their writings as high as twenty thousand dollars a year and there are some authors, rare ones, who make from fifty to seventy-five thousand dollars a year from their writings; and some of the most successful authors in some of their most successful years have made as high as a hundred thousand dollars or two hundred thousand dollars.

Personally, it strikes me that the one great special advantage of authorship as a means of livelihood is that it gives one more freedom than is given any person in business or in the various other professions. The author's advice and business is under his hat and he can go anywhere and write anywhere as the spirit moves him.

Thanking you for your good letter,
Sincerely yours,
Jack London

Glen Ellen, Calif.
Feb. 5, 1915

My dear Ethel Jennings:

In reply to yours of January 12th, 1915:

By the way, January 12th, 1915 was my birthday—39 years old, if you please.

I am returning you herewith your manuscript. First of all, just a few words as to your story. A reader who knew nothing about you and who read your story in a book or magazine would wonder for a long time after beginning as to what part of the world was the locality of your story. You should have worked in artistically, and as a germane part of the story, right near the start, the locality of the story.

Your story, really, had no locality. Your story had no place as being distinctively different from any other place of the earth's surface. This is your first mistake in the story.

Let me tell you another mistake which I get from your letter, namely that you wrote this story at white heat. Never write any story at white heat. Hell is kept warm by unpublished manuscripts that were written at white heat.

Develop your locality. Get in your local color. Develop your characters. Make your characters real to your readers. Get out of yourself and into your reader's minds and know what impression your readers are getting from your written words. Always remember that you are not writing for yourself but that you are writing for your readers. In connection with this let me recommend to you Herbert Spencer's "Philosophy of Style." You should be able to find this essay, "The Philosophy of Style," in Herbert Spencer's collected works in any public library.

On page 3 of your manuscript you stop and tell the reader how awful it is for a woman to live with a man outside of wedlock. I am perfectly willing to grant that it is awful for a woman to live with a man outside of wedlock, but as an artist I am compelled to tell you for heaven's sake, don't stop your story in order to tell your reader how awful it is. Let your reader get this sense of awfulness from your story as your story goes on.

Further I shall not go with you in discussing your manuscript with you except to tell you that no magazine or newspaper in the United States would accept your story as it now stands.

It has long been a habit of mine to have poems typed off in duplicate which I may send to my friends. I am sending you a few samples of said poems that I have on hand at the present time. I am sending them to you in order that you may study them carefully and try to know the fineness of utterance, the new and strong and beautiful way of expressing old, eternal things which always appear apparently as new things to new eyes who try to convey what they see to the new generations.

I am enclosing you also a letter to a young writer, a letter that I was compelled to write the other day. His situation is somewhat different from yours and yet the same fundamental truth and conditions underrun his situation and your situation. In line with this let me suggest that you study always the goods that are being bought by the magazines. These goods that the magazines publish are the marketable goods. If you want to sell such goods you must write marketable goods. Any time that you are down in this part of California look up Mrs. London and me on the ranch and I can tell you more in ten minutes than I can write you in ten years.

Sincerely yours,
Jack London

ROBERT LOUIS STEVENSON (1850–94)

"ON SOME TECHNICAL ELEMENTS OF STYLE IN LITERATURE"

Born on November 13, 1850 in Edinburgh, Scotland, Robert Louis Stevenson began his study of writing at the University of Edinburgh by imitating such masters as William Hazlitt, Daniel Defoe, and Michel de Montaigne. Although Stevenson's first major work, a travelogue entitled *An Inland Voyage*, was published in 1878, he did not achieve lasting commercial success until five years later with the publication of *Treasure Island* in 1883, and later with *Kidnapped* and *The Strange Case of Dr. Jekyll and Mr. Hyde* in 1888. Although Stevenson's popularity waxed and waned throughout the twentieth century, he has of late ascended in the literary canon and is considered one of the finest writers of English neo-romanticism. He is also an enduring favorite of readers around the world. In 1890, Stevenson purchased a large piece of land on Upolu, in the Samoan Islands, where he died four years later at the age of forty-four.

"On Some Technical Elements of Style in Literature," one of the most straightforward and practical essays in this collection, is an analysis of prose writing, intended for no other purpose than enhancing the skills of the amateur writer. To this end, Stevenson discusses word choice, the patterns of phrases, rhythm, and content. The piece provides a valuable lesson on the uses of language by a writer who, as G. K. Chesterton wrote, "seemed to pick the right word up on the point of his pen, like a man playing spillikins."

There is nothing more disenchanting to man than to be shown the springs and mechanism of any art. All our arts and occupations lie wholly on the surface; it is on the surface that we perceive their beauty, fitness, and significance; and to pry below is to be appalled by their emptiness and shocked by the coarseness of the strings and pulleys. In a similar way, psychology

itself, when pushed to any nicety, discovers an abhorrent bald-
ness, but rather from the fault of our analysis than from any
poverty native to the mind. And perhaps in aesthetics the reason
is the same: those disclosures which seem fatal to the dignity of
art seem so perhaps only in the proportion of our ignorance; and
those conscious and unconscious artifices which it seems
unworthy of the serious artist to employ were yet, if we had the
power to trace them to their springs, indications of a delicacy of
the sense finer than we conceive, and hints of ancient harmonies
in nature. This ignorance at least is largely irremediable. We
shall never learn the affinities of beauty, for they lie too deep in
nature and too far back in the mysterious history of man. The
amateur, in consequence, will always grudgingly receive details
of method, which can be stated but never can wholly be
explained; nay, on the principle laid down in *Hudibras,* that—

> Still the less they understand,
> The more they admire the sleight-of-hand,

many are conscious at each new disclosure of a diminution in
the ardour of their pleasure. I must therefore warn that well-
known character, the general reader, that I am here embarked
upon a most distasteful business: taking down the picture from
the wall and looking on the back; and, like the inquiring child,
pulling the musical cart to pieces.

1. Choice of Words

The art of literature stands apart from among its sisters,
because the material in which the literary artist works is the
dialect of life; hence, on the one hand, a strange freshness and
immediacy of address to the public mind, which is ready
prepared to understand it; but hence, on the other, a singular
limitation. The sister arts enjoy the use of a plastic and ductile
material, like the modeller's clay; literature alone is condemned
to work in mosaic with finite and quite rigid words. You have
seen these blocks, dear to the nursery: this one a pillar, that a
pediment, a third a window or a vase. It is with blocks of just
such arbitrary size and figure that the literary architect is condemned to design the palace of his art. Nor is this all; for since

these blocks, or words, are the acknowledged currency of our daily affairs, there are here possible none of those suppressions by which other arts obtain relief, continuity, and vigour: no hieroglyphic touch, no smoothed impasto, no inscrutable shadow, as in painting; no blank wall, as in architecture; but every word, phrase, sentence, and paragraph must move in a logical progression, and convey a definite conventional import.

Now the first merit which attracts in the pages of a good writer, or the talk of a brilliant conversationalist, is the apt choice and contrast of the words employed. It is, indeed, a strange art to take these blocks, rudely conceived for the purpose of the market or the bar, and by tact of application touch them to the finest meanings and distinctions, restore to them their primal energy, wittily shift them to another issue, or make of them a drum to rouse the passions. But though this form of merit is without doubt the most sensible and seizing, it is far from being equally present in all writers. The effect of words in Shakespeare, their singular justice, significance, and poetic charm, is different, indeed, from the effect of words in Addison or Fielding. Or, to take an example nearer home, the words in Carlyle seem electrified into an energy of lineament, like the faces of men furiously moved; whilst the words in Macaulay, apt enough to convey his meaning, harmonious enough in sound, yet glide from the memory like undistinguished elements in a general effect. But the first class of writers have no monopoly of literary merit. There is a sense in which Addison is superior to Carlyle; a sense in which Cicero is better than Tacitus, in which Voltaire excels Montaigne: it certainly lies not in the choice of words; it lies not in the interest or value of the matter; it lies not in force of intellect, of poetry, or of humour. The three first are but infants to the three second; and yet each, in a particular point of literary art, excels his superior in the whole. What is that point?

2. THE WEB

Literature, although it stands apart by reason of the great destiny and general use of its medium in the affairs of men, is yet an art like other arts. Of these we may distinguish two great classes:

those arts, like sculpture, painting, acting, which are representative, or, as used to be said very clumsily, imitative; and those, like architecture, music, and the dance, which are self-sufficient, and merely presentative. Each class, in right of this distinction, obeys principles apart; yet both may claim a common ground of existence, and it may be said with sufficient justice that the motive and end of any art whatever is to make a pattern; a pattern, it may be, of colours, of sounds, of changing attitudes, geometrical figures, or imitative lines; but still a pattern. That is the plane on which these sisters meet; it is by this that they are arts; and if it be well they should at times forget their childish origin, addressing their intelligence to virile tasks, and performing unconsciously that necessary function of their life, to make a pattern, it is still imperative that the pattern shall be made.

Music and literature, the two temporal arts, contrive their pattern of sounds in time; or, in other words, of sounds and pauses. Communication may be made in broken words, the business of life be carried on with substantives alone; but that is not what we call literature; and the true business of the literary artist is to plait or weave his meaning, involving it around itself; so that each sentence, by successive phrases, shall first come into a kind of knot, and then, after a moment of suspended meaning, solve and clear itself. In every properly constructed sentence there should be observed this knot or hitch; so that (however delicately) we are led to foresee, to expect, and then to welcome the successive phrases. The pleasure may be heightened by an element of surprise, as, very grossly, in the common figure of the antithesis, or, with much greater subtlety, where an antithesis is first suggested and then deftly evaded. Each phrase, besides, is to be comely in itself; and between the implication and the evolution of the sentence there should be a satisfying equipoise of sound; for nothing more often disappoints the ear than a sentence solemnly and sonorously prepared, and hastily and weakly finished. Nor should the balance be too striking and exact, for the one rule is to be infinitely various; to interest, to disappoint, to surprise, and yet still to gratify; to be ever changing, as it were, the stitch, and yet still to give the effect of an ingenious neatness.

The conjurer juggles with two oranges, and our pleasure in beholding him springs from this, that neither is for an instant overlooked or sacrificed. So with the writer. His pattern, which is to please the supersensual ear, is yet addressed, throughout and first of all, to the demands of logic. Whatever be the obscurities, whatever the intricacies of the argument, the neatness of the fabric must not suffer, or the artist has been proved unequal to his design. And, on the other hand, no form of words must be selected, no knot must be tied among the phrases, unless knot and word be precisely what is wanted to forward and illuminate the argument; for to fail in this is to swindle in the game. The genius of prose rejects the *cheville* no less emphatically than the laws of verse; and the *cheville,* I should perhaps explain to some of my readers, is any meaningless or very watered phrase employed to strike a balance in the sound. Pattern and argument live in each other; and it is by the brevity, clearness, charm, or emphasis of the second, that we judge the strength and fitness of the first.

Style is synthetic; and the artist, seeking, so to speak, a peg to plait about, takes up at once two or more elements or two or more views of the subject in hand; combines, implicates, and contrasts them; and while, in one sense, he was merely seeking an occasion for the necessary knot, he will be found, in the other, to have greatly enriched the meaning, or to have transacted the work of two sentences in the space of one. In the change from the successive shallow statements of the old chronicler to the dense and luminous flow of highly synthetic narrative, there is implied a vast amount of both philosophy and wit. The philosophy we clearly see, recognising in the synthetic writer a far more deep and stimulating view of life, and a far keener sense of the generation and affinity of events. The wit we might imagine to be lost; but it is not so, for it is just that wit, these perpetual nice contrivances, these difficulties overcome, this double purpose attained, these two oranges kept simultaneously dancing in the air, that, consciously or not, afford the reader his delight. Nay, and this wit, so little recognised, is the necessary organ of that philosophy which we so much admire. That style is therefore the most perfect, not, as fools say, which is the most natural, for the most natural is the disjointed babble of the chronicler; but which attains the highest degree of elegant and pregnant implication unobtrusively; or if obtrusively, then with the greatest gain to sense and vigour. Even the derangement of the phrases from their (so-called) natural order is luminous for the mind; and it is by the means of such designed reversal that the elements of a judgment may be most pertinently marshalled, or the stages of a complicated action most perspicuously bound into one.

The web, then, or the pattern: a web at once sensuous and logical, an elegant and pregnant texture: that is style, that is the foundation of the art of literature. Books indeed continue to be read, for the interest of the fact or fable, in which this quality is poorly represented, but still it will be there. And, on the other hand, how many do we continue to peruse and reperuse with pleasure whose only merit is the elegance of texture? I am tempted to mention Cicero; and since Mr. Anthony Trollope is dead, I will. It is a poor diet for the mind, a very colourless and toothless "criticism of life"; but we enjoy the pleasure of a most intricate and dexterous pattern, every stitch a model at once of elegance and of good sense; and the two oranges, even if one of them be rotten, kept dancing with inimitable grace.

Up to this moment I have had my eye mainly upon prose; for though in verse also the implication of the logical texture is a crowning beauty, yet in verse it may be dispensed with. You would think that here was a death-blow to all I have been saying; and far from that, it is but a new illustration of the principle involved. For if the versifier is not bound to weave a pattern of his own, it is because another pattern has been formally imposed upon him by the laws of verse. For that is the essence of a prosody. Verse may be rhythmical; it may be merely alliterative; it may, like the French, depend wholly on the (quasi) regular recurrence of the rhyme; or, like the Hebrew, it may consist in the strangely fanciful device of repeating the same idea. It does not matter on what principle the law is based, so it be a law. It may be pure convention; it may have no inherent beauty; all that we have a right to ask of any prosody is, that it shall lay down a pattern for the writer, and that what it lays down shall be neither too easy nor too hard. Hence it comes that it is much easier for men of equal facility to write fairly pleasing verse than reasonably interesting prose; for in prose the pattern itself has to be invented, and the difficulties first created before they can be solved. Hence, again, there follows the peculiar greatness of the true versifier: such as Shakespeare, Milton, and Victor Hugo, whom I place beside them as versifier merely, not as poet. These not only knit and knot the logical texture of the style with all the dexterity and strength of prose; they not only fill up the pattern of the verse with infinite variety and sober wit; but they give us, besides, a rare and special pleasure, by the art, comparable to that of counterpoint, with which they follow at the same time, and now contrast, and now combine, the double pattern of the texture and the verse. Here the sounding line concludes; a little further on, the well-knit sentence; and yet a little further, and both will reach their solution on the same ringing syllable. The best that can be offered by the best writer of prose is to show us the development of the idea and the stylistic pattern proceed hand in hand, sometimes by an obvious and triumphant effort, sometimes with a great air of ease and nature. The writer of verse, by virtue of conquering another difficulty, delights us with a new series of triumphs. He follows three purposes where his rival followed only two; and the change is of precisely the same nature as that from melody to harmony. Or if you prefer to return to the juggler, behold him now, to the vastly increased enthusiasm of the spectators, juggling with three oranges instead of two. Thus it is: added difficulty, added beauty; and the pattern, with every fresh element, becoming more interesting in itself.

Yet it must not be thought that verse is simply an addition; something is lost as well as something gained; and there remains plainly traceable, in comparing the best prose with the best verse, a certain broad distinction of method in the web. Tight as the versifier may draw the knot of logic, yet for the ear he still leaves the tissue of the sentence floating somewhat loose. In prose, the sentence turns upon a pivot, nicely balanced, and fits into itself with an obtrusive neatness like a puzzle. The ear remarks and is singly gratified by this return and balance; while in verse it is all diverted to the measure. To find comparable passages is hard; for either the versifier is hugely the superior of the rival, or, if he be not, and still persist in his more delicate enterprise, he fails to be as widely his inferior. But let us select them from the pages of the same writer, one who was ambidexter; let us take, for instance, Rumour's Prologue to the Second Part of *Henry IV,* a fine flourish of eloquence in Shakespeare's second manner, and set it side by side with Falstaff's praise of sherris, (act iv, scene iii); or let us compare the beautiful prose spoken throughout by Rosalind and Orlando; compare, for example, the first speech of all, Orlando's speech to Adam, with what passage it shall please you to select—the Seven Ages from the same play, or even such a stave of nobility as Othello's farewell to war; and still you will be able to perceive, if you have an ear for that class of music, a certain superior degree of organisation in the prose; a compacter fitting of the parts; a balance in the swing and the return as of a throbbing pendulum. We must not, in things temporal, take from those who have little, the little that they have; the merits of prose are inferior, but they are not the same; it is a little kingdom, but an independent.

3. Rhythm of the Phrase

Some way back, I used a word which still awaits an application. Each phrase, I said, was to be comely; but what is a comely phrase? In all ideal and material points, literature, being a representative art, must look for analogies to painting and the like; but in what is technical and executive, being a temporal art, it must seek for them in music. Each phrase of each sentence, like an air or a recitative in music, should be so artfully compounded out of long and short, out of accented and unaccented, as to gratify the sensual ear. And of this the ear is the sole judge. It is impossible to lay down laws. Even in our accentual and rhythmic language no analysis can find the secret of the beauty of a verse; how much less, then, of those phrases, such as prose is built of, which obey no law but to be lawless and yet to please? The little that we know of verse (and for my part I owe it all to my friend Professor Fleeming Jenkin) is, however, particularly interesting in the present connection. We have been accustomed to describe the heroic line as five iambic feet, and to be filled with pain and confusion whenever, as by the conscientious schoolboy, we have heard our own description put in practice.

All night | the dreàd | less àn | gel ùn | pursùed,[2]

goes the schoolboy; but though we close our ears, we cling to our definition, in spite of its proved and naked insufficiency. Mr. Jenkin was not so easily pleased, and readily discovered that the heroic line consists of four groups, or, if you prefer the phrase, contains four pauses:

All night | the dreadless | angel | unpursued.

Four groups, each practically uttered as one word: the first, in this case, an iamb; the second, an amphibrachys; the third, a trochee; and the fourth, an amphimacer; and yet our schoolboy, with no other liberty but that of inflicting pain, had triumphantly scanned it as five iambs. Perceive, now, this fresh richness of intricacy in the web; this fourth orange, hitherto unremarked, but still kept flying with the others. What had seemed to be one thing it now appears is two; and, like some puzzle in arithmetic, the verse is made at the same time to read in fives and to read in fours.

But again, four is not necessary. We do not, indeed, find verses in six groups, because there is not room for six in the ten syllables; and we do not find verses of two, because one of the main distinctions of verse from prose resides in the comparative shortness of the group; but it is even common to find verses of three. Five is the one forbidden number; because five is the number of the feet; and if five were chosen, the two patterns would coincide, and that opposition which is the life of verse would instantly be lost. We have here a clue to the effect of polysyllables, above all in Latin, where they are so common and make so brave an architecture in the verse; for the polysyllable is a group of Nature's making. If but some Roman would return from Hades (Martial, for choice), and tell me by what conduct of the voice these thundering verses should be uttered—"*Aut*

---

2. Milton.

Lacedaemonium Tarentum," for a case in point—I feel as if I should enter at last into the full enjoyment of the best of human verses.

But, again, the five feet are all iambic, or supposed to be; by the mere count of syllables the four groups cannot be all iambic; as a question of elegance, I doubt if any one of them requires to be so; and I am certain that for choice no two of them should scan the same. The singular beauty of the verse analysed above is due, so far as analysis can carry us, part, indeed, to the clever repetition of L, D, and N, but part to this variety of scansion in the groups. The groups which, like the bar in music, break up the verse for utterance, fall uniambically; and in declaiming a so-called iambic verse, it may so happen that we never utter one iambic foot. And yet to this neglect of the original beat there is a limit.

Athens, the eye of Greece, mother of arts,[3]

is, with all its eccentricities, a good heroic line; for though it scarcely can be said to indicate the beat of the iamb, it certainly suggests no other measure to the ear. But begin—

Mother Athens, eye of Greece,

or merely "Mother Athens," and the game is up, for the trochaic beat has been suggested. The eccentric scansion of the groups is an adornment; but as soon as the original beat has been forgotten, they cease implicitly to be eccentric. Variety is what is sought; but if we destroy the original mould, one of the terms of this variety is lost, and we fall back on sameness. Thus, both as to the arithmetical measure of the verse, and the degree of regularity in scansion, we see the laws of prosody to have one common purpose: to keep alive the opposition of two schemes simultaneously followed; to keep them notably apart, though still coincident; and to balance them with such judicial nicety before the reader, that neither shall be unperceived and neither signally prevail.

The rule of rhythm in prose is not so intricate. Here, too, we

3. Milton.

write in groups, or phrases, as I prefer to call them, for the prose phrase is greatly longer and is much more nonchalantly uttered than the group in verse; so that not only is there a greater interval of continuous sound between the pauses, but, for that very reason, word is linked more readily to word by a more summary enunciation. Still, the phrase is the strict analogue of the group, and successive phrases, like successive groups, must differ openly in length and rhythm. The rule of scansion in verse is to suggest no measure but the one in hand; in prose, to suggest no measure at all. Prose must be rhythmical, and it may be as much so as you will; but it must not be metrical. It may be anything, but it must not be verse. A single heroic line may very well pass and not disturb the somewhat larger stride of the prose style; but one following another will produce an instant impression of poverty, flatness, and disenchantment. The same lines delivered with the measured utterance of verse would perhaps seem rich in variety. By the more summary enunciation proper to prose, as to a more distant vision, these niceties of difference are lost. A whole verse is uttered as one phrase; and the ear is soon wearied by a succession of groups identical in length. The prose writer, in fact, since he is allowed to be so much less harmonious, is condemned to a perpetually fresh variety of movement on a larger scale, and must never disappoint the ear by the trot of an accepted metre. And this obligation is the third orange with which he has to juggle, the third quality which the prose writer must work into his pattern of words. It may be thought perhaps that this is a quality of ease rather than a fresh difficulty; but such is the inherently rhythmical strain of the English language, that the bad writer—and must I take for example that admired friend of my boyhood, Captain Reid?—the inexperienced writer, as Dickens in his earlier attempts to be impressive, and the jaded writer, as any one may see for himself, all tend to fall at once into the production of bad blank verse. And here it may be pertinently asked, Why bad? And I suppose it might be enough to answer that no man ever made good verse by accident, and that no verse can ever sound otherwise than trivial when uttered with the delivery of prose. But we can go beyond such answers. The weak side of verse is the regularity of the

beat, which in itself is decidedly less impressive than the movement of the nobler prose; and it is just into this weak side, and
this alone, that our careless writer falls. A peculiar density and
mass, consequent on the nearness of the pauses, is one of the
chief good qualities of verse; but this our accidental versifier,
still following after the swift gait and large gestures of prose,
does not so much as aspire to imitate. Lastly, since he remains
unconscious that he is making verse at all, it can never occur to
him to extract those effects of counterpoint and opposition
which I have referred to as the final grace and justification of
verse, and, I may add, of blank verse in particular.

4. Contents of the Phrase

Here is a great deal of talk about rhythm—and naturally; for
in our canorous language rhythm is always at the door. But it
must not be forgotten that in some languages this element is
almost, if not quite, extinct, and that in our own it is probably
decaying. The even speech of many educated Americans sounds
the note of danger. I should see it go with something as bitter as
despair, but I should not be desperate. As in verse no element,
not even rhythm, is necessary, so, in prose also, other sorts of
beauty will arise and take the place and play the part of those
that we outlive. The beauty of the expected beat in verse, the
beauty in prose of its larger and more lawless melody, patent as
they are to English hearing, are already silent in the ears of our
next neighbours; for in France the oratorical accent and the pattern of the web have almost or altogether succeeded to their
places; and the French prose writer would be astounded at the
labours of his brother across the Channel, and how a good quarter of his toil, above all *invita Minerva,* is to avoid writing verse.
So wonderfully far apart have races wandered in spirit, and so
hard it is to understand the literature next door!

Yet French prose is distinctly better than English; and French
verse, above all while Hugo lives, it will not do to place upon one
side. What is more to our purpose, a phrase or a verse in French
is easily distinguishable as comely or uncomely. There is then
another element of comeliness hitherto overlooked in this
analysis: the contents of the phrase. Each phrase in literature is

built of sounds, as each phrase in music consists of notes. One sound suggests, echoes, demands, and harmonises with another; and the art of rightly using these concordances is the final art in literature. It used to be a piece of good advice to all young writers to avoid alliteration; and the advice was sound, in so far as it prevented daubing. None the less for that, was it abominable nonsense, and the mere raving of those blindest of the blind who will not see. The beauty of the contents of a phrase, or of a sentence, depends implicitly upon alliteration and upon assonance. The vowel demands to be repeated; the consonant demands to be repeated; and both cry aloud to be perpetually varied. You may follow the adventures of a letter through any passage that has particularly pleased you; find it, perhaps, denied a while, to tantalise the ear; find it fired again at you in a whole broadside; or find it pass into congenerous sounds, one liquid or labial melting away into another. And you will find another and much stranger circumstance. Literature is written by and for two senses: a sort of internal ear, quick to perceive "unheard melodies"; and the eye, which directs the pen and deciphers the printed phrase. Well, even as there are rhymes for the eye, so you will find that there are assonances and alliterations; that where an author is running the open A, deceived by the eye and our strange English spelling, he will often show a tenderness for the flat A; and that where he is running a particular consonant, he will not improbably rejoice to write it down even when it is mute or bears a different value.

Here, then, we have a fresh pattern—a pattern, to speak grossly, of letters—which makes the fourth preoccupation of the prose writer, and the fifth of the versifier. At times it is very delicate and hard to perceive, and then perhaps most excellent and winning (I say perhaps); but at times again the elements of this literal melody stand more boldly forward and usurp the ear. It becomes, therefore, somewhat a matter of conscience to select examples; and as I cannot very well ask the reader to help me, I shall do the next best by giving him the reason or the history of each selection. The two first, one in prose, one in verse, I chose without previous analysis, simply as engaging passages that had long re-echoed in my ear.

I cannot praise a fugitive and cloistered virtue, unexercised and unbreathed, that never sallies out and sees her adversary, but slinks out of the race where that immortal garland is to be run for, not without dust and heat.[4]

Down to "virtue," the current S and R are both announced and repeated unobtrusively, and by way of a grace-note that almost inseparable group PVF is given entire.[5] The next phrase is a period of repose, almost ugly in itself, both S and R still audible, and B given as the last fulfilment of PVF. In the next four phrases, from "that never" down to "run for," the mask is thrown off, and, but for a slight repetition of the F and V, the whole matter turns, almost too obtrusively, on S and R; first S coming to the front, and then R.

In the concluding phrase all these favourite letters, and even the flat A, a timid preference for which is just perceptible, are discarded at a blow and in a bundle; and to make the break more obvious, every word ends with a dental, and all but one with T, for which we have been cautiously prepared since the beginning. The singular dignity of the first clause, and this hammer-stroke of the last, go far to make the charm of this exquisite sentence. But it is fair to own that S and R are used a little coarsely.

In Xanady did Kubla Khan	(KANDL)
A stately pleasure dome decree,	(KDLSR)
Where Alph the sacred river ran,	(KANDLSR)
Through caverns measureless to man,	(KANLSR)
Down to a sunless sea.[6]	(NDLS)

Here I have put the analysis of the main group alongside the lines; and the more it is looked at, the more interesting it will seem. But there are further niceties. In lines two and four, the current S is most delicately varied with Z. In line three, the cur-

---

4. Milton.
5. As PVF will continue to haunt us through our English examples, take, by way of comparison, this Latin verse, of which it forms a chief adornment, and do not hold me answerable for the all too Roman freedom of the sense: "*Hanc volo, quae facilis, quae palliolata vagatur.*"
6. Coleridge.

rent flat A is twice varied with the open A, already suggested in line two, and both times ("where" and "sacred") in conjunction with the current R. In the same line F and V (a harmony in themselves, even when shorn of their comrade P) are admirably contrasted. And in line four there is a marked subsidiary M, which again was announced in line two. I stop from weariness, for more might yet be said.

My next example was recently quoted from Shakespeare as an example of the poet's colour sense. Now, I do not think litera-ture has anything to do with colour, or poets anyway the better of such a sense; and I instantly attacked this passage, since "pur-ple" was the word that had so pleased the writer of the article, to see if there might not be some literary reason for its use. It will be seen that I succeeded amply; and I am bound to say I think the passage exceptional in Shakespeare—exceptional, indeed, in literature; but it was not I who chose it.

> The BaRge she sat iN, like a BURNished throNe
> BURNT oN the water: the POOP was BeateN gold,
> PURPle the sails and so PUR° Fumèd that
> The wiNds were love-sick with them.[7]

It may be asked why I have put the F of "perfumèd" in capi-tals; and I reply, because this change from P to F is the comple-tion of that from B to P, already so adroitly carried out. Indeed, the whole passage is a monument of curious ingenuity; and it seems scarce worth while to indicate the subsidiary S, L, and W. In the same article, a second passage from Shakespeare was quoted, once again as an example of his colour sense:

> A mole cinque-spotted like the crimson drops
> I' the bottom of a cowslip.[8]

It is very curious, very artificial, and not worth while to analyse at length: I leave it to the reader. But before I turn my back on Shakespeare, I should like to quote a passage, for my own pleasure, and for a very model of every technical art:

---

7. *Antony and Cleopatra.*
8. *Cymbeline.*

But in the wind and tempest of her frown,
W. P. V.[9] F. (st) (ow)
Distinction with a loud and powerful fan,
W.P. F. (st) (ow) L.

Puffing at all, winnows the light away;
W. P. F. L.
And what hath mass and matter by itself
W. F. L. M. A.
Lies rich in virtue and unmingled.[10]
V. L. M.

From these delicate and choice writers I turned with some curiosity to a player of the big drum—Macaulay. I had in hand the two-volume edition, and I opened at the beginning of the second volume. Here was what I read:

> "The violence of revolutions is generally proportioned to the degree of the maladministration which has produced them. It is therefore not strange that the government of Scotland, having been during many years greatly more corrupt than the government of England, should have fallen with a far heavier ruin. The movement against the last king of the house of Stuart was in England conservative, in Scotland destructive. The English complained not of the law, but of the violation of the law."

This was plain-sailing enough; it was our old friend PVF, floated by the liquids in a body; but as I read on, and turned the page, and still found PVF with his attendant liquids, I confess my mind misgave me utterly. This could be no trick of Macaulay's; it must be the nature of the English tongue. In a kind of despair, I turned half-way through the volume; and coming upon his lordship dealing with General Cannon, and fresh from Claverhouse and Killiecrankie, here, with elucidative spelling, was my reward:

> "Meanwhile the disorders of Kannon's Kamp went on inKreasing. He Kalled a Kouncil of war to Konsider what Kourse it would be advisable to taKe. But as soon as the Kouncil had met, a preliminary Kuestion was raised. The army was almost eKsKlusively a Highland army. The recent vKktory had been won eKsKlusively by Highland warriors. Great chiefs who had brought siKs or Seven hundred fighting men into the field did

9. The V is in "of."
10. *Troilus and Cressida.*

not think it fair that they should be outvoted by gentlemen from Ireland, and from the Low Kountries, who bore indeed King James's Kommission, and were Kalled Kolonels and Kaptains, but who were Kolonels without regiments and Kaptains without Kompanies."

A moment of FV in all this world of K's! It was not the English language, then, that was an instrument of one string, but Macaulay that was an incomparable dauber.

It was probably from this barbaric love of repeating the same sound, rather than from any design of clearness, that he acquired his irritating habit of repeating words; I say the one rather than the other, because such a trick of the ear is deeper-seated and more original in man than any logical consideration. Few writers, indeed, are probably conscious of the length to which they push this melody of letters. One, writing very diligently, and only concerned about the meaning of his words and the rhythm of his phrases, was struck into amazement by the eager triumph with which he cancelled one expression to substitute another. Neither changed the sense; both being monosyllables, neither could affect the scansion; and it was only by looking back on what he had already written that the mystery was solved: the second word contained an open A, and for nearly half a page he had been riding that vowel to the death.

In practice, I should add, the ear is not always so exacting; and ordinary writers, in ordinary moments, content themselves with avoiding what is harsh, and here and there, upon a rare occasion, buttressing a phrase, or linking two together, with a patch of assonance or a momentary jingle of alliteration. To understand how constant is this preoccupation of good writers, even where its results are least obtrusive, it is only necessary to turn to the bad. There, indeed, you will find cacophony supreme, the rattle of incongruous consonants only relieved by the jaw-breaking hiatus, and whole phrases not to be articulated by the powers of man.

CONCLUSION

We may now briefly enumerate the elements of style. We have, peculiar to the prose writer, the task of keeping his phrases large, rhythmical, and pleasing to the ear, without ever allowing them to fall into the strictly metrical: peculiar to the versifier, the task of combining and contrasting his double, treble, and quadruple pattern, feet and groups, logic and metre—harmonious in diversity: common to both, the task of artfully combining the prime elements of language into phrases that shall be musical in the mouth; the task of weaving their argument into a texture of committed phrases and of rounded periods—but this particularly binding in the case of prose: and, again common to both, the task of choosing apt, explicit, and communicative words. We begin to see now what an intricate affair is any perfect passage; how many faculties, whether of taste or pure reason, must be held upon the stretch to make it; and why, when it is made, it should afford us so complete a pleasure. From the arrangement of according letters, which is altogether arabesque and sensual, up to the architecture of the elegant and pregnant sentence, which is a vigorous act of the pure intellect, there is scarce a faculty in man but has been exercised. We need not wonder, then, if perfect sentences are rare, and perfect pages rarer.

(1905)

WILLA CATHER (1873–1947)

"ON THE ART OF FICTION"

Willa Cather was born on December 7, 1873 in Virginia's Shenandoah Valley. She lived there until the age of nine, when her family moved to Red Cloud, Nebraska—the frontier town that would become the setting for many of her novels. Cather first began writing at the University of Nebraska, where she showed impressive talent in journalism and fiction. Upon graduation, she spent a few years editing and writing at magazines such as the *Pittsburgh Leader* and *McClure's*, before deciding to focus solely on fiction. Although her first novel *Alexander's Bridge* (1912) chronicled life in the big city, it was not until she turned to her Nebraska roots for inspiration—on the advice of friend Sarah Orne Jewett—that Cather found lasting literary success with *O! Pioneers* (1913), *My Antonia* (1918), and *One of Ours* (1922), which won her the Pulitzer Prize in 1923.

Willa Cather's short essay, "On the Art of Fiction," was first written for *The Borzoi* in 1920. In it, she discusses the primary obstacles confronting young writers at that time. In the process of exploring the pitfalls and how to avoid them, Cather offers her own philosophy of art and writing which is as relevant to aspiring writers today as it was then.

One is sometimes asked about the "obstacles" that confront young writers who are trying to do good work. I should say the greatest obstacles that writers today have to get over are the dazzling journalistic successes of twenty years ago, stories that surprised and delighted by their sharp photographic detail and that were really nothing more than lively pieces of reporting. The whole aim of that school of writing was novelty—never a very important thing in art. They gave us, altogether, poor standards—taught us to multiply our ideas instead of to condense them. They tried to make a story out of every theme that occurred to them and to get returns on every situation that suggested itself. They got returns, of a kind. But their work, when one looks back on it, now that the novelty upon which they counted so much is gone, is journalistic and thin. The especial merit of a good reportorial story is that it shall be intensely interesting and pertinent today and shall have lost its point by tomorrow.

Art, it seems to me, should simplify. That, indeed, is very nearly the whole of the higher artistic process; finding what conventions of form and what detail one can do without and yet preserve the spirit of the whole—so that all that one has suppressed and cut away is there to the reader's consciousness as much as if it were in type on the page. Millet had done hundreds of sketches of peasants sowing grain, some of them very complicated and interesting, but when he came to paint the spirit of them all into one picture, "The Sower," the composition is so simple that it seems inevitable. All the discarded sketches that went before made the picture what it finally became, and the process was all the time one of simplifying, of sacrificing many conceptions good in themselves for one that was better and more universal.

Any first-rate novel or story must have in it the strength of a dozen fairly good stories that have been sacrificed to it. A good workman can't be a cheap workman; he can't be stingy about wasting material, and he cannot compromise. Writing ought either to be the manufacture of stories for which there is a market demand—a business as safe and commendable as making soap or breakfast foods—or it should be an art, which is always a search for something for which there is no market demand, something new and untried, where the values are intrinsic and have nothing to do with standardized values. The courage to go on without compromise does not come to a writer all at once— nor, for that matter, does the ability. Both are phases of natural development. In the beginning, the artist, like his public, is wedded to old forms, old ideals, and his vision is blurred by the memory of old delights he would like to recapture.

(1920)

SINCLAIR LEWIS (1885–1951)

"HOW I WROTE A NOVEL ON THE TRAIN AND BESIDE THE KITCHEN SINK"

Sinclair Lewis, born Harry Sinclair Lewis in Sauk City, Minnesota in 1885, began his writing career shortly after graduating from Yale University in 1908. Lewis's first novel, *Hike and the Aeroplane*, was published in 1912, under the pseudonym Tom Graham. Although he went on to publish five more critically acclaimed novels in the next seven years, Lewis did not attain great popularity until the publication of *Main Street* in 1920. At once a critique of both American provincialism and American intellectualism, *Main Street* sold over 250,000 copies during its first six months in print, bringing Lewis considerable prominence. His next two books, *Babbitt* and *Arrowsmith*, were huge successes as well, with Lewis receiving the 1926 Pulitzer Prize for the latter—an honor he refused. As he explained in a 1926 letter: "Every compulsion is put upon writers to become safe, polite, obedient, and sterile. In protest, I . . . decline the Pulitzer Prize." Sinclair Lewis went on to produce a total of twenty-two novels and three plays, and in 1930 he became the first American ever to receive the Nobel Prize in Literature.

Lewis wrote the following essay one year after the publication of *Main Street*, at the height of his renown. It was inspired by the people who had, over the years, sought advice from him about how to "break into the magazine game." As such, it offers a variety of recommendations, from the sincere to the satirical. And more than anything else, it admonishes the would-be writer to stop making excuses, sit down, and write. In Lewis's own words: "Make black marks on white paper. That little detail of writing is one that is neglected by almost all the aspirants I meet."

I have a philosophical principle, a handy and portable key to achievement, for the twenty or thirty million young Americans who at the present second are wondering how they can attain it. It applies to shoemakers as much as to authors. It is: Six times one equals six. It sounds simple and rather foolish, and it is harder to carry out than an altitude flight.

Being a professional writer, not a good one but quite a hard-working one, I hear at least once a week, "What's the trick? How can I break into the magazine game? I want to write. I've been reading your stuff, and I think I could do something like it. What must I do?"

My first answer is, "Well, you can save a great deal of time by not reading my stuff. Read Thomas Hardy, Conrad, Anatole France. Or, if you want the younger men, look at Joseph Hergesheimer, James Branch Cabell, Henry Mencken; and all of these astonishing young Englishmen—Walpole, Maugham, Cannan, Lawrence, and the rest."

The achievement hunter ferrets an ancient envelope out of his pocket and solemnly notes down the names, as though they were magic formulas, and I have a private fit of despair in the most convenient corner, because young men who solemnly note down things rarely put their notes into life. And, to defend my own sex, let me say that frequently the young man in question is a young woman. One out of every three women of any leisure will, without much pressing, confide that she "wants to write"—not to write anything in particular, but just write.

After restoring the annotated envelope to a pocket where it will be lost for keeps, he, or she, confides that he—confound those pronouns—they confide that they are peculiar, quite different from all other humans, because, by the most extraordinary circumstances, they "haven't much time."

The young newspaperman boasts that after a night at the grind, he is tired. And he says it with a haughty air of being the only person on the entire earth and suburban planets who works hard enough to get tired. And a young married woman tranquilly asserts that after a conference with cook, a bridge-tea, laboring at eating dinner, and watching the nurse put baby to bed, and is so exhausted that she cannot possibly carry out her acute ambition to write.

I want to add to recorded history the fact that there is no patent on being tired and no monopoly in it. Several people have been tired since the days of Assyria. It is not so novel a state that it is worth much publicity. When I hear of a marvelous news case of it on the part of a yearner, I sigh:

"But do you really want to write?"

"Oh, yessssss!"

"Why?"

"Oh, it must be such a fascinating life."

"Huh!" the boorish professional grunts, "I don't see anything very fascinating about sitting before a typewriter six or seven hours a day."

"Oh, yes, but the—the joy of self-expression, and the fame."

"Fame! Huh! I'll lay you nine to one that if Rudyard Kipling and Jack Dempsey arrived on the same train, Kipling wouldn't even be able to hire a taxi."

"I don't *care*," the yearner insists. "I think my present life is intolerably dull, and I do want to write."

"Very well then. I'll tell you the trick. You have to do only one thing: Make black marks on white paper. That little detail of writing is one that is neglected by almost all the aspirants I meet."

He—and especially she—is horribly disappointed by my cynicism. He—and often she—finds nothing interesting in making marks on paper. What he, she, it, they, and sometimes W and Y, want to do is to sit dreaming purple visions, and have them automatically appear: (1) on a manuscript; (2) on a check from the editor. So he, and the rest of the pronouns, usually finds the same clever excuse:

"But I simply can't seem to find the time. Oh, I just lonnnnnnnnng to write, but when I sit down to it, someone always comes and disturbs me, and I'm so tired, and— Well, I always tell Adolphus that some day I'll have six months free, and I'll devote them to writing, and then I just know I'll succeed. I always say to Dolph, I know I can write better stuff than I read in all these magazines."

"Look here. Could you get an hour free every day?"

After a certain amount of bullying, they usually admit the hour. The newspaper reporter who desires to follow Irv Cobb confesses that he could make use of an hour while he is waiting for an assignment. The young housewife who wishes to produce a volume of fairy stories for children—and 96.3 per cent of all young housewives do so wish—grants that if she hustled a little with her sewing and marketing and telephoning to other housewives, she could have an hour free.

"All right!" the discouraging philosopher concludes, "an hour a day for six days is six hours a week, twenty-five or so hours a month. Anybody who is not deaf, blind, and addicted to *dementia praecox,* can write between a hundred and a thousand words an hour. Making it a minimum of a hundred, you can do five thousand words in two months—and that is a fair-sized short story. At the maximum of a thousand, you could do a short story in a week.

"Very few writers produce more than one short story a month, in the long average, though they can use as much as they wish of twenty-four hours a day. That is because they become wearied of invention, of planning new stories; must spur themselves by the refreshment and recreation of real life. But that real life you are getting all day. You have, as far as time goes, just as much chance as they. If you concentrate an hour a day you can produce somewhere between half as much as, and four times as much as, a professional writer.

"Providing always—providing you can write. And providing you have enough will power to use your ability. And providing you stop deceiving yourself about not having the time!"

Six times one is six, in hours as much as in the potatoes which William is always selling to John in the problem. But you can vary the multiplication. Of those few people who cannot control an hour a day, there are probably none above the mental grade of *moron* who cannot get in a quarter of an hour daily. If the aspirant actually is too tired at night, he can get up a quarter of an hour earlier in the morning.

If a man wrote only twenty-five words a day, but kept that up for twelve years, he would have a full-length novel. Twelve years for one novel will seem slow to the get-literary-quick yearners. Yet most good writers toil through fifteen or twenty years of apprenticeship before they succeed, and a scholar thinks nothing of twenty years spent on a work of research which does well if it sells a thousand copies.

If you have it in you to produce one thundering good novel, one really big novel, just one, your place in American literature will be safe for the next hundred years. For very few even of the well-known novelists ever produce as much as one thoroughly good novel in all their lives, and still fewer produce more than one. You can rival or excel them with twenty-five words a day— if you have the ability—and *if you really want to.* If you haven't the ability, and if you don't violently want to, then you couldn't do it with twenty-four hours free every day.

But once you understand this principle, you must also grasp another thing: the need of concentration. Each daily hour must instantly hook on the hour of the day before. Concentration can be learned—and without any trick exercises. It is largely habit. The taxi-driver, calm and concentrated in traffic that would shatter an amateur, the policeman attending strictly to the crowd and ignoring the king driving by, the button maker serene on the job all day long—none of them are heroic exceptions, but all of them are practicing excellent concentration. It can be learned—if you want to. But for heaven's sake, if you don't sufficiently want to, stop yearning for the almost entirely imaginary glories of the literary career.

Now, if all of this applied only to writing, it would scarce be worth recording. But it happened to apply equally to the ambition of almost every young man or woman, whether that ambition is the study of law, the designing of new types of airplanes—or of hats—the mastery of business detail, or gaining promotion and greater knowledge in your present work, your present office or shop.

A large percentage of people go on vaguely believing that they would like to be lawyers or executives, vaguely desiring to do something about it, vaguely talking about it, vaguely excusing themselves. And the years slip on, treacherous and swift and cruel; and by and by they are seventy, and the chance has gone—for want of understanding that six times one daily hour is six hours every week.

But let me tremulously endeavor to remove myself from the category of chest-pounding, imitate-me-and-you-will-be-successful inspiration-mongers by hastening to admit that I have had many years of laziness. I have beat the job in about all the known ways. Jack Dunnigan fired me from the San Francisco *Bulletin* because I was a rotten reporter; and with amazing unanimity Charley Kloeber fired me from the Associated Press. But there did come a time when I desperately saw that if I was ever going to be free to write, I must—write!

I, too, "had no time for it." I was, by now, a rather busy editor for a publishing firm. I read manuscripts, saw authors and artists, answered telephone calls from the printer, wrote advertising, devised devilish ways of getting publicity, from nine-fifteen to five or six or seven, with forty miles a day of commuting besides. And, like the complainants of whom I complain, I was dead tired every evening—too tired to think of anything but the Krazy Kat pictures and the inviting genius of the man who invented sleeping.

So I decided that I would not have time for being tired, instead of not having time for writing.

I wrote practically all of a novel on trains, and the rest of it I wrote at times when I didn't have time to write!

About one morning a week—not oftener, I confess—I had courage enough to get up an hour earlier than usual. Our Long Island bungalow took an hour to heat after the furnace had been fed; but the kitchen was warm, and before the cook arrived from her palatial mansion I got in most of an hour of writing—with the drain board in the kitchen as my desk!

Between adjectives I made a cup of coffee on the gas range. By request, my wife did not get up to make it for me. I wanted to concentrate on the job. And I may say that no studio—I believe there are writers who have things called studios—and no Hepplewhite chairs and Spanish tapestries and Sheraton desks ever made a better environment for writing than a drain board, with a cup of coffee steaming beside me in the sink.

There was an hour a week, at least; and that was fifty hours a year.

Commuting into New York took from thirty-five to fifty minutes. I finished the morning paper in seven or eight minutes, and after that I did not, as invariably I wanted to, gossip about golf, the water rates, and Tammany with my fellow commuters.

I looked around, got ready to be queer, hauled out a plain manila filing folder, and began to write in pencil, with the folder on my knee as a desk. I got from fifty to five hundred words done almost every morning.

There are many paragraphs in *The Trail of the Hawk*—probably the only arousing ones in that not very interesting novel—which were composed in order to give a good bewildered time to some shoe merchant or broker sitting beside me in the train. At first their ponderously cautious curiosity bothered me, but as I gradually got the habit of concentration, it amused me.

Returning on the train at night, I was usually too tired to write again, but sometimes I did manage five minutes. And when I lunched alone I found that I could plan two or three days' work without having to "find time." I don't know that thinking about story plots took any longer than meditating on the impossibility of finding time to think about plots.

In the evening, after dinner and playing and loafing and perhaps reading a manuscript not finished in office hours, I could usually capture another hour or two. Oh, I didn't want to work. I was tired. I longed to go to bed. But I didn't let myself do it till midnight.

Nor did Saturday afternoon have to be devoted entirely to tramping or tennis or a swim. I compromised. I was home by one; wrote for two hours; then enjoyed ten times more the beautiful freedom of a hike across the Long Island hills.

A lot of you, my dear young friends, whose candid faces I see here before me tonight—and let me say that I am always glad to get back to your beautiful little city, the loveliest spot on my entire Lyceum circuit—many of you will endeavor to avoid my prosaic principle of six times one is six by turning virtuous; by quoting some of my predecessors on this platform, and stating in pure and ringing accents that you can't write, or read law, or design frocks, or study for promotion in the office, at six-thirty A.M., on the drain board, because that would be unfair to your present job.

I have yet to learn why excited, future-reaching, adventurous work at your real ambition should be more injurious to your job than sitting up half the night to play poker, or gossiping in a smoke-filled room till you are a pulp of aimlessness, or painstakingly cooking fudge, or yawning at a sentimental movie full of domestic virtues and kitties, or industriously reading the social column in a newspaper.

Oh, I've been guilty. I've dawdled through the movies, sat talking about things that did not interest me with people who bored me—because it was too much trouble to shake them off and go home. The last time I committed these two faults in one evening was something less than twenty-four hours before striking out these majestic chords on the typewriter.

But at least I have learned this: When I have not done the things I thought I wanted to do; if, in the future, I shall not do the things I now think I want to do, the one excuse I may *not* use is: "I can't find the time." I have, and you have, twenty-four hours a day. And that is, so far as I can find out, approximately the same amount of daily time that was granted to Michelangelo, Pasteur, Shakespeare, or Ty Cobb.

"I want to write." Well then, hang it—write!

If you decide that the one way to do the job is to do it, kindly get through it without the use of any of the following words: Pep, punch, jazz, hustle, snap, virile, and, most of all, red-blooded.

These words are the symbols of what may well be the worst fault in American philosophy—a belief that a shallow appearance of energy actually is energy. In begging people to use the selvages and scraps of their time, I wish them to understand that I am not advocating the Pep creed: that religion of making a lot of noise about what you're going to do as soon as you can take time off from making a lot of noise.

There is no Pep, there is no phonographic bellowing of the cant phrases of the marketplace, in a quiet, resolute desire for daily concentration. In fact, the man who pounds his desk, and scatters papers all over the floor, and yells at the telephone operator, and bursts into flights of optimism, has no time to settle down to the job.

To the man with a sense of humor, this clamorous insistence on violently hustling nowhere in particular, and standing on one's hind legs to advocate that form of activity as contributing to the welfare of the nation, is simply impossible. To the man with a passionate desire for beauty, with a longing to build—whether it is to build novels or stone walls or shoes—there is only shrinking disgust at the yapping of the man whose entire creed is: "What you guys want to do is to jazz up the business and keep the iron men doing quick turnovers."

The real disciple of success is diligent about the Lord's affairs, yet he is curiously gentle. He uses his reason. And he does something more subtle than merely spending his spare quarter-hours in working for advancement. He thinks. Most people do not actively think about anything beyond the immediate details of food and the job. For it is not easy to detach one's self from pleased self-approbation and to see clearly one's relation to the round of life.

The builder, and he may be a builder in business as much as in any art, concentrates on his building, yet sees all of life expanding, as circle beyond circle of possible achievement is disclosed. He will neither whine, "I can't find time," nor, at the other extreme, will he pound his own back and bellow, "Oh, I'm one grand little worker." His idol is neither the young man sighing over a listless pipe, nor the human calliope. He works, persistently, swiftly, without jar.

(1921)

MARK TWAIN (1835–1910)

"MY LITERARY SHIPYARD"

Born Samuel Langhorne Clemens in 1835, Mark Twain began writing at the age of sixteen while working as an apprentice printer in his hometown of Hannibal, Missouri. After a few years of working at printers, on riverboats, and as a miner, Twain got his first real job as a writer at the *Daily Territorial Enterprise*, a newspaper in Virginia City, Nevada. Although he can claim to be one of the most prolific of all American writers, Twain will always be best remembered for his iconic novel, *The Adventures of Huckleberry Finn*, as well as *The Adventures of Tom Sawyer*, *The Prince and the Pauper*, and *A Connecticut Yankee in King Arthur's Court*. As Ernest Hemingway aptly wrote of him, "All modern American literature comes from one book by Mark Twain called *Huckleberry Finn* . . . All American writing comes from that. There was nothing before. There has been nothing as good since."

In the following essay, published posthumously in 1922, Twain discusses how he is able to finish a piece of fiction when he arrives at a roadblock and the story stops "writing itself." He sets aside the story, sometimes for years, until the time comes for it to write itself once again. The reader will find here many sound ideas about how to transcend some of the many obstacles that interfere with the creative writing process.

There has never been a time in the past thirty-five years when my literary shipyard hadn't two or more half-finished ships on the ways, neglected and baking in the sun; generally there have been three or four. This has an unbusinesslike look, but it was not purposeless, it was intentional. As long as a book would write itself, I was a faithful and interested amanuensis, and my industry did not flag; but the minute that the book tried to shift to *my* head the labor of contriving its situations, inventing its adventures and conducting its conversations, I put it away and dropped it out of my mind. Then I examined my unfinished properties to see if among them there might not be one whose interest in itself had revived, through a couple of years' restful idleness, and was ready to take me on again as amanuensis.

It was by accident that I found out that a book is pretty sure to get tired along about the middle, and refuse to go on with its work until its powers and its interest should have been refreshed by a rest and its depleted stock of raw materials reinforced by lapse of time. It was when I had reached the middle of *Tom Sawyer* that I made this invaluable find. At page 400 of my manuscript the story made a sudden and determined halt and refused to proceed another step. Day after day it still refused. I was disappointed, distressed, and immeasurably astonished, for I knew quite well that the tale was not finished, and I could not understand why I was not able to go on with it. The reason was very simple—my tank had run dry; it was empty; the stock of materials in it was exhausted; the story could not go on without materials; it could not be wrought out of nothing. When the manuscript had lain in a pigeon-hole two years I took it out one day, and read the last chapter that I had written. It was then that I made the great discovery that when the tank runs dry you've only to leave it alone and it will fill up again, in time, while you are asleep—also while you are at work at other things, and are quite unaware that this unconscious and profitable cerebration is going on. There was plenty of material now, and the book went on and finished itself without any trouble.

Ever since then, when I have been writing a book I have pigeon-holed it without misgivings when its tank ran dry, well knowing that it would fill up again without any of my help within the next two or three years, and that then the work of completing it would be simple and easy. *The Prince and the Pauper* struck work in the middle, because the tank was dry, and I did not touch it again for two years. A dry interval of two years occurred in *The Connecticut Yankee at the Court of King Arthur.* A like interval has occurred in the middle of other books of mine. Two similar intervals have occurred in a story of mine called "Which Was It?" In fact, the second interval has gone considerably over time, for it is now four years since that second one intruded itself. I am sure that the tank is full again now, and that I could take up that book and write the other half of it without a break or any lapse of interest—but I sha'n't do it. The pen is irksome to me. I was born lazy, and dictating has spoiled me. I am quite sure I shall never touch a pen again; therefore that book will remain unfinished—a pity, too, for the idea of it is new and would spring a handsome surprise upon the reader at the end.

There is another unfinished book, which I should probably entitle *The Refuge of the Derelicts*. It is half finished and will remain so. There is still another one, entitled *The Adventure of a Microbe During Three Thousand Years; by a Microbe*. It is half finished and will remain so. There is yet another—*The Mysterious Stranger*. It is more than half finished. I would dearly like to finish it, and it causes me a real pang to reflect that it is not to be. These several tanks are full now, and those books would go gaily along and complete themselves if I would hold the pen, but I am tired of the pen.

There was another of these half-finished stories. I carried it as far as thirty-eight thousand words four years ago, then destroyed it for fear I might some day finish it. Huck Finn was the teller of the story, and of course Tom Sawyer and Jim were the heroes of it. But I believed that that trio had done work enough in this world and were entitled to a permanent rest.

In Rouen in '93 I destroyed fifteen thousand dollars' worth of manuscript; and in Paris, in the beginning of '94, I destroyed ten thousand dollars' worth—I mean, estimated as magazine stuff. I was afraid to keep those piles of manuscript on hand, lest I be tempted to sell them, for I was fairly well persuaded that they were not up to the standard. Ordinarily there would have been no temptation present, and I would not think of publishing doubtful stuff—but I was heavily in debt then, and the temptation to mend my condition was so strong that I burned the manuscript to get rid of it. My wife not only made no objection, but encouraged me to do it, for she cared more for my reputation than for any other concern of ours. About that time she helped me put another temptation behind me. This was an offer of sixteen thousand dollars a year, for five years, to let my name be used as editor of a humorous periodical. I praise her for furnishing her help in resisting that temptation, for it is her due. There was no temptation about it, in fact, but she would have offered her help just the same if there had been one. I can conceive of many wild and extravagant things when my imagination is in good repair, but I can conceive of nothing quite so wild and extravagant as the idea of my accepting the editorship of a humorous periodical. I should regard that as the saddest of all occupations. If I should undertake it I should have to add to it the occupation of undertaker, to relieve it in some degree of its cheerlessness.

There are some books that refuse to be written. They stand their ground, year after year, and will not be persuaded. It isn't because the book is not there and worth being written—it is only because the right form for the story does not present itself. There is only one right form for a story, and if you fail to find that form the story will not tell itself. You may try a dozen wrong forms, but in each case you will not get very far before you discover that you have not found the right one—then that story will always stop and decline to go any farther. In the story of *Joan of Arc* I made six wrong starts, and each time that I offered the result to Mrs. Clemens she responded with the same deadly criticism—silence. She didn't say a word, but her silence spoke with the voice of thunder. When at last I found the right form I recognized at once that it was the right one, and I knew what she would say. She said it, without doubt or hesitation.

In the course of twelve years I made six attempts to tell a simple little story which I knew would tell itself in four hours if I could ever find the right starting-point. I scored six failures; then one day in London I offered the text of the story to Robert McClure, and proposed that he publish that text in the magazine and offer a prize to the person who should tell it best. I became greatly interested and went on talking upon the text for half an hour; then he said:

"You have told the story yourself. You have nothing to do but put in on paper just as you have told it."

I recognized that this was true. At the end of four hours it was finished, and quite to my satisfaction. So it took twelve years and four hours to produce that little bit of a story, which I have called "The Death Wafer."

To start right is certainly an essential. I have proved this too many times to doubt it. Twenty-five or thirty years ago I began a story which was to turn upon the marvels of mental telegraphy. A man was to invent a scheme whereby he could synchronize two minds, thousands of miles apart, and enable them to freely converse together through the air without the aid of a wire. Four times I started it in the wrong way, and it wouldn't go. Three times I discovered my mistake after writing about a hundred pages. I discovered it the fourth time when I had written four hundred pages—then I gave it up and put the whole thing in the fire.

(1922)

RAYMOND CHANDLER (1888–1959)

"THE SIMPLE ART OF MURDER"

Born in Chicago in 1888, Raymond Chandler moved with his mother to Great Britain in 1895 shortly after his parents' divorce. It was there, while a student at Dulwich College, that Chandler acquired his love of language and literature, publishing his first poem "The Unknown Love" in 1908. It wasn't until 1933—after many years of working odd jobs in California—that Chandler's first pulp fiction story "Blackmailers Don't Shoot," published in *Black Mask* magazine, kicked off his career as a preeminent crime writer. However, it was the 1939 publication of *The Big Sleep* that earned Chandler his place as a writer not only of pulp fiction, but of great literature as well. His razor-sharp prose and hardboiled style was admired and emulated by writers of the stature of Ian Fleming and Evelyn Waugh.

Like Conrad's preface, "The Simple Art of Murder" is as much a manifesto as it is an essay on writing. Unflinching in the demands he makes on fiction to be realistic and believable, Chandler analyzes detective fiction from Christie to Hammett, eschewing anything that does not achieve the standards he has set for literature as a whole. More importantly, Chandler offers a set of criteria and a method of assessment which any writer can apply both to what they read and to what they write.

Fiction in any form has always intended to be realistic. Old-fashioned novels which now seem stilted and artificial to the point of burlesque did not appear that way to the people who first read them. Writers like Fielding and Smollett could seem realistic in the modern sense because they dealt largely with uninhibited characters, many of whom were about two jumps ahead of the police, but Jane Austen's chronicles of highly inhibited people against a background of rural gentility seem real enough psychologically. There is plenty of that kind of social and emotional hypocrisy around today. Add to it a liberal dose of intellectual pretentiousness and you get the tone of the book page in your daily paper and the earnest and fatuous atmosphere breathed by discussion groups in little clubs. These are the people who make best sellers, which are promotional jobs based on a sort of indirect snob appeal, carefully escorted by the trained seals of the critical fraternity, and lovingly tended and watered by certain much too powerful pressure groups whose business is selling books, although they would like you to think they are fostering culture. Just get a little behind in your payments and you will find out how idealistic they are.

The detective story for a variety of reasons can seldom be promoted. It is usually about murder and hence lacks the element of uplift. Murder, which is a frustration of the individual and hence a frustration of the race, may have, and in fact has, a good deal of sociological implication. But it has been going on too long for it to be news. If the mystery novel is at all realistic (which it very seldom is) it is written in a certain spirit of detachment; otherwise nobody but a psychopath would want to write it or read it. The murder novel has also a depressing way of minding its own business, solving its own problems and answering its own questions. There is nothing left to discuss, except whether it was well enough written to be good fiction, and the people who make up the half-million sales wouldn't know that anyway. The detection of quality in writing is difficult enough even for those who make a career of the job, without paying too much attention to the matter of advance sales.

The detective story (perhaps I had better call it that, since the English formula still dominates the trade) has to find its public by a slow process of distillation. That it does do this, and holds on thereafter with such tenacity, is a fact; the reasons for it are a study for more patient minds than mine. Nor is it any part of my thesis to maintain that it is a vital and significant form of art. There are no vital and significant forms of art; there is only art, and precious little of that. The growth of populations has in no way increased the amount; it has merely increased the adeptness with which substitutes can be produced and packaged.

Yet the detective story, even in its most conventional form, is difficult to write well. Good specimens of the art are much rarer than good serious novels. Second-rate items outlast most of the high-velocity fiction, and a great many that should never have been born simply refuse to die at all. They are as durable as the statues in public parks and just about as dull.

This fact is annoying to people of what is called discernment. They do not like it that penetrating and important works of fiction of a few years back stand on their special shelf in the library marked "Best-sellers of Yesteryear" or something, and nobody goes near them but an occasional shortsighted customer who bends down, peers briefly and hurries away; while at the same time old ladies jostle each other at the mystery shelf to grab off some item of the same vintage with such a title as *The Triple Petunia Murder Case* or *Inspector Pinchbottle to the Rescue.* They do not like it at all that "really important books" (and some of them are too, in a way) get the frosty mitt at the reprint counter while *Death Wears Yellow Garters* is put out in editions of fifty or one hundred thousand copies on the newsstands of the country, and is obviously not there just to say goodbye.

To tell the truth, I do not like it very much myself. In my less stilted moments I too write detective stories, and all this immortality makes just a little too much competition. Even Einstein couldn't get very far if three hundred treatises of the higher physics were published every year, and several thousand others in some form or other were hanging around in excellent condition, and being read too.

Hemingway says somewhere that the good writer competes only with dead. The good detective story writer (there must after all be a few) competes not only with all the unburied dead but with all the hosts of the living as well. And on almost equal terms; for it is one of the qualities of this kind of writing that the thing that makes people read it never goes out of style. The hero's tie may be a little out of the mode and the good gray inspector may arrive in a dogcart instead of a streamlined sedan with siren screaming, but what he does when he gets there is the same old futzing around with timetables and bits of charred paper and who trampled the jolly old flowering arbutus under the library window.

I have, however, a less sordid interest in the matter. It seems to me that production of detective stories on so large a scale, and by writers whose immediate reward is small and whose meed of critical praise is almost nil, would not be possible at all if the job took any talent. In that sense the raised eyebrow of the critic and the shoddy merchandising of the publisher are perfectly logical. The average detective story is probably no worse than the average novel, but you never see the average novel. It doesn't get published. The average—or only slightly above average—detective story does. Not only is it published but it is sold in small quantities to rental libraries and it is read. There are even a few optimists who buy it at the full retail price of two dollars, because it looks so fresh and new and there is a picture of a corpse on the cover.

And the strange thing is that this average, more than middling dull, pooped-out piece of utterly unreal and mechanical fiction is really not very different from what are called the masterpieces of the art. It drags on a little more slowly, the dialogue is a shade grayer, the cardboard out of which the characters are cut is a shade thinner, and the cheating is a little more obvious. But it is the same kind of book. Whereas the good novel is not at all the same kind of book as the bad novel. It is about entirely different things. But the good detective story and the bad detective story are about exactly the same things, and they are about them in very much the same way. There are reasons for this too, and reasons for the reasons; there always are.

I suppose the principal dilemma of the traditional or classic or straight deductive or logic and deduction novel of detection is that for any approach to perfection it demands a combination of qualities not found in the same mind. The coolheaded constructionist does not also come across with lively characters, sharp dialogue, a sense of pace, and an acute use of observed detail. The grim logician has as much atmosphere as a drawing board. The scientific sleuth has a nice new shiny laboratory, but I'm sorry I can't remember the face. The fellow who can write you a vivid and colorful prose simply will not be bothered with the coolie labor of breaking down unbreakable alibis. The master of rare knowledge is living psychologically in the age of the hoop skirt. If you know all you should know about ceramics and Egyptian needlework, you don't know anything at all about the police. If you know that platinum won't melt under about 3000°F. by itself, but will melt at the glance of a pair of deep blue eyes if you put it near a bar of lead, then you don't know how men make love in the twentieth century. And if you know enough about the elegant *flânerie* of the prewar French Riviera to lay your story in that locale, you don't know that a couple of capsules of barbital small enough to be swallowed will not only not kill a man—they will not even put him to sleep if he fights against them.

Every detective story writer makes mistakes, of course, and none will ever know as much as he should. Conan Doyle made mistakes which completely invalidated some of his stories, but he was a pioneer, and Sherlock Holmes after all is mostly an attitude and a few dozen lines of unforgettable dialogue. It is the ladies and gentlemen of what Mr. Howard Haycraft (in his book *Murder for Pleasure*) calls the Golden Age of detective fiction that really get me down. This age is not remote. For Mr. Haycraft's purpose it starts after the First World War and lasts up to about 1930. For all practical purposes it is still here. Two thirds or three quarters of all the detective stories published still adhere to the formula the giants of this era created, perfected, polished, and sold to the world as problems in logic and deduction.

These are stern words, but be not alarmed. They are only words. Let us glance at one of the glories of the literature, an acknowledged masterpiece of the art of fooling the reader without cheating him. It is called *The Red House Mystery*, was written by A. A. Milne, and has been named by Alexander Woollcott (rather a fast man with a superlative) "one of the three best mystery stories of all time." Words of that size are not spoken lightly. The book was published in 1922 but is timeless, and might as easily have been published in July, 1939, or, with a few slight changes, last week. It ran thirteen editions and seems to have been in print, in the original format, for about sixteen years. That happens to few books of any kind. It is an agreeable book, light, amusing in the *Punch* style, written with a deceptive smoothness that is not so easy as it looks.

It concerns Mark Ablett's impersonation of his brother Robert as a hoax on his friends. Mark is the owner of the Red House, a typical laburnum-and-lodge-gate English country house. He has a secretary who encourages him and abets him in this impersonation, and who is going to murder him if he pulls it off. Nobody around the Red House has ever seen Robert, fifteen years absent in Australia and known by repute as a nogood. A letter is talked about (but never shown) announcing Robert's arrival, and Mark hints it will not be a pleasant occasion. One afternoon, then, the supposed Robert arrives, identifies himself to a couple of servants, is shown into the study. Mark goes in after him (according to testimony at the inquest). Robert is then found dead on the floor with a bullet hole in his face, and of course Mark has vanished into thin air. Arrive the police, who suspect Mark must be the murderer, remove the débris, and proceed with the investigation—and in due course, with the inquest.

Milne is aware of one very difficult hurdle and tries as well as he can to get over it. Since the secretary is going to murder Mark, once Mark has established himself as Robert, the impersonation has to continue and fool the police. Since, also, everybody around the Red House knows Mark intimately, disguise is necessary. This is achieved by shaving off Mark's beard, roughening his hands ("not the hands of a manicured gentleman"—testimony), and the use of a gruff voice and rough manner.

But this is not enough. The cops are going to have the body and the clothes on it and whatever is in the pockets. Therefore none of this must suggest Mark. Milne therefore works like a switch engine to put over the motivation that Mark is such a thoroughly conceited performer that he dresses the part down to the socks and underwear (from all of which the secretary has removed the maker's labels), like a ham blacking himself all over to play Othello. If the reader will buy this (and the sales record shows he must have), Milne figures he is solid. Yet, however light in texture the story may be, it is offered as a problem of logic and deduction.

If it is not that, it is nothing at all. There is nothing else for it to be. If the situation is false, you cannot even accept it as a light novel, for there is no story for the light novel to be about. If the problem does not contain the elements of truth and plausibility, it is no problem; if the logic is an illusion, there is nothing to deduce. If the impersonation is impossible once the reader is told the conditions it must fulfill, then the whole thing is a fraud. Not a deliberate fraud, because Milne would not have written the story if he had known what he was up against. He is up against a number of deadly things, none of which he even considers. Nor, apparently, does the casual reader, who wants to like the story—hence takes it at its face value. But the reader is not called upon to know the facts of life when the author does not. The author is the expert in the case.

Here is what this author ignores:

1. The coroner holds formal jury inquest on a body for which no legal competent identification is offered. A coroner, usually in a big city, will sometimes hold inquest on a body that *cannot* be identified, if the record of such an inquest has or may have a value (fire, disaster, evidence of murder). No such reason exists here, and there is no one to identify the body. Witnesses said the man said he was Robert Ablett. This is mere presumption, and has weight only if nothing conflicts with it. Identification is a condition precedent to an inquest. It is a matter of law. Even in death a man has a right to his own identity. The coroner will, wherever humanly possible, enforce that right. To neglect it would be a violation of his office.

2. Since Mark Ablett, missing and suspected of the murder, cannot defend himself, all evidence of his movements before and after the murder is vital (as also whether he has money to run away on); yet all such evidence is given by the man closest to the murder and is without corroboration. It is automatically suspect until proved true.

3. The police find by direct investigation that Robert Ablett was not well thought of in his native village. Somebody there must have known him. No such person was brought to the inquest. (The story couldn't stand it.)

4. The police know there is an element of threat in Robert's

supposed visit, and that it is connected with the murder must be obvious to them. Yet they make no attempt to check Robert in Australia, or find out what character he had there, or what associates, or even if he actually came to England, and with whom. (If they had, they would have found out he had been dead three years.)

5. The police surgeon examines a body with a recently shaved beard (exposing unweathered skin) and artificially roughened hands, but it is the body of a wealthy, soft-living man, long resident in a cool climate. Robert was a rough individual and had lived fifteen years in Australia. That is the surgeon's information. It is impossible he would have noticed nothing to conflict with it.

6. The clothes are nameless, empty, and have had the labels removed. Yet the man wearing them asserted an identity. The presumption that he was not what he said he was is overpowering. Nothing whatever is done about his peculiar circumstance. It is never even mentioned as being peculiar.

7. A man is missing, a well-known local man, and a body in the morgue closely resembles him. It is impossible that the police should not at once eliminate the chance that the missing man *is* the dead man. Nothing would be easier than to prove it. Not even to think of it is incredible. It makes idiots of the police, so that a brash amateur may startle the world with a fake solution.

The detective in the case is an insouciant amateur named Anthony Gillingham, a nice lad with a cheery eye, a nice little flat in town, and that airy manner. He is not making any money on the assignment, but is always available when the local gendarmerie loses its notebook. The English police endure him with their customary stoicism, but I shudder to think what the boys down at the Homicide Bureau in my city would do to him.

There are even less plausible examples of the art than this. In *Trent's Last Case* (often called "the perfect detective story") you have to accept the premise that a giant of international finance, whose lightest frown makes Wall Street quiver like a chihuahua, will plot his own death so as to hang his secretary, and that the secretary when pinched will maintain an aristocratic silence—

the old Etonian in him, maybe. I have known relatively few international financiers, but I rather think the author of this novel has (if possible) known fewer.

There is another one, by Freeman Wills Crofts (the soundest builder of them all when he doesn't get too fancy), wherein a murderer, by the aid of make-up, split-second timing and some very sweet evasive action, impersonates the man he has just killed and thereby gets him alive and distant from the place of the crime. There is one by Dorothy Sayers in which a man is murdered alone at night in his house by a mechanically released weight which works because he always turns the radio on at just such a moment, always stands in just such a position in front of it, and always bends over just so far. A couple of inches either way and the customers would get a rain check. This is what is vulgarly known as having God sit in your lap; a murderer who needs that much help from Providence must be in the wrong business.

And there is a scheme of Agatha Christie's featuring M. Hercule Poirot, that ingenious Belgian who talks in a literal translation of school-boy French. By duly messing around with his "little gray cells" M. Poirot decides that since nobody on a certain through sleeper could have done the murder alone, everybody did it together, breaking the process down into a series of simple operations like assembling an egg beater. This is the type that is guaranteed to knock the keenest mind for a loop. Only a halfwit could guess it.

There are much better plots by these same writers and by others of their school. There may be one somewhere that would really stand up under close scrutiny. It would be fun to read it, even if I did have to go back to page 47 and refresh my memory about exactly what time the second gardener potted the prize-winning tea-rose begonia. There is nothing new about these stories and nothing old. The ones I mentioned are all English because the authorities, such as they are, seem to feel that the English writers had an edge in this dreary routine and that the Americans, even the creator of Philo Vance, only make the Junior Varsity.

This, the classic detective story, has learned nothing and forgotten nothing. It is the story you will find almost any week in the big shiny magazines, handsomely illustrated, and paying due deference to virginal love and the right kind of luxury goods. Perhaps the tempo has become a trifle faster and the dialogue a little more glib. There are more frozen daiquiris and stingers and fewer glasses of crusty old port, more clothes by *Vogue* and décors by *House Beautiful,* more chic, but not more truth. We spend more time in Miami hotels and Cape Cod summer colonies and go not so often down by the old gray sundial in the Elizabethan garden.

But fundamentally it is the same careful grouping of suspects, the same utterly incomprehensible trick of how somebody stabbed. Mrs. Pottington Postlethwaite III with the solid platinum poniard just as she flatted on the top note of the "Bell Song" from *Lakmé* in the presence of fifteen ill-assorted guests; the same ingénue in fur-trimmed pajamas screaming in the night to make the company pop in and out of doors and ball up the timetable; the same moody silence next day as they sit around sipping Singapore slings and sneering at each other, while the flatfeet crawl to and fro under the Persian rugs, with their derby hats on.

Personally I like the English style better. It is not quite so brittle and the people as a rule just wear clothes and drink drinks. There is more sense of background, as if Cheesecake Manor really existed all around and not just in the part the camera sees; there are more long walks over the downs and the characters don't all try to behave as if they had just been tested by MGM. The English may not always be the best writers in the world, but they are incomparably the best dull writers.

There is a very simple statement to be made about all these stories: they do not really come off intellectually as problems, and they do not come off artistically as fiction. They are too contrived, and too little aware of what goes on in the world. They try to be honest, but honesty is an art. The poor writer is dishonest without knowing it, and the fairly good one can be dishonest because he doesn't know what to be honest about. He thinks a complicated murder scheme which baffled the lazy reader, who won't be bothered itemizing the details, will also baffle the police, whose business is with details.

The boys with their feet on the desks know that the easiest murder case in the world to break is the one somebody tried to get very cute with; the one that really bothers them is the murder somebody thought of only two minutes before he pulled it off. But if the writers of this fiction wrote about the kind of murders that happen, they would also have to write about the authentic flavor of life as it is lived. And since they cannot do that, they pretend that what they do is what should be done. Which is begging the question—and the best of them know it.

In her introduction to the first *Omnibus of Crime*, Dorothy Sayers wrote: "It [the detective story] does not, and by hypothesis never can, attain the loftiest level of literary achievement." And she suggested somewhere else that this is because it is a "literature of escape" and not "a literature of expression." I do not know what the loftiest level of literary achievement is: neither did Aeschylus or Shakespeare; neither does Miss Sayers. Other things being equal, which they never are, a more powerful theme will provoke a more powerful performance. Yet some very dull books have been written about God, and some very fine ones about how to make a living and stay fairly honest. It is always a matter of who writes the stuff, and what he has in him to write it with.

As for "literature of expression" and "literature of escape"— this is critics' jargon, a use of abstract words as if they had absolute meanings. Everything written with vitality expresses that vitality: there are no dull subjects, only dull minds. All men who read escape from something else into what lies behind the printed page; the quality of the dream may be argued, but its release has become a functional necessity. All men must escape at times from the deadly rhythm of their private thoughts. It is part of the process of life among thinking beings. It is one of the things that distinguish them from the three-toed sloth; he apparently—one can never be quite sure—is perfectly content hanging upside down on a branch, not even reading Walter Lippmann. I hold no particular brief for the detective story as the ideal escape. I merely say that *all* reading for pleasure is escape, whether it be Greek, mathematics, astronomy, Benedetto Croce, or *The Diary of the Forgotten Man.* To say otherwise is to be an intellectual snob, and a juvenile at the art of living.

I do not think such considerations moved Miss Dorothy Sayers to her essay in critical futility.

I think what was really gnawing at Miss Sayers' mind was the slow realization that her kind of detective story was an arid formula which could not even satisfy its own implications. It was second-grade literature because it was not about the things that could make first-grade literature. If it started out to be about real people (and she could write about them—her minor characters show that), they must very soon do unreal things in order to form the artificial pattern required by the plot. When they did unreal things, they ceased to be real themselves. They became puppets and cardboard lovers and papier-mâché villains and detectives of exquisite and impossible gentility.

The only kind of writer who could be happy with these properties was the one who did not know what reality was. Dorothy Sayers' own stories show that she was annoyed by this triteness; the weakest element in them is the part that makes them detective stories, the strongest the part which could be removed without touching the "problem of logic and deduction." Yet she could not or would not give her characters their heads and let them make their own mystery. It took a much simpler and more direct mind than hers to do that.

In *The Long Week End,* which is a drastically competent account of English life and manners in the decades following the First World War, Robert Graves and Alan Hodge gave some attention to the detective story. They were just as traditionally English as the ornaments of the Golden Age, and they wrote of the time in which these writers were almost as well known as any writers in the world. Their books in one form or another sold into the millions, and in a dozen languages. These were the people who fixed the form and established the rules and founded the famous Detection Club, which is a Parnassus of English writers of mystery. Its roster includes practically every important writer of detective fiction since Conan Doyle.

But Graves and Hodge decided that during this whole period only one first-class writer had written detective stories at all. An American, Dashiell Hammett. Traditional or not, Graves and Hodge were not fuddyduddy connoisseurs of the second-rate; they could see what went on in the world and that the detective story of their time didn't; and they were aware that writers who have the vision and the ability to produce real fiction do not produce unreal fiction.

How original a writer Hammett really was it isn't easy to decide now, even if it mattered. He was one of a group—the only one who achieved critical recognition—who wrote or tried to write realistic mystery fiction. All literary movements are like this; some one individual is picked out to represent the whole movement; he is usually the culmination of the movement. Hammett was the ace performer, but there is nothing in his work that is not implicit in the early novels and short stories of Hemingway.

Yet, for all I know, Hemingway may have learned something from Hammett as well as from writers like Dreiser, Ring Lardner, Carl Sandburg, Sherwood Anderson, and himself. A rather revolutionary debunking of both the language and the material of fiction had been going on for some time. It probably started in poetry; almost everything does. You can take it clear back to Walt Whitman, if you like. But Hammett applied it to the detective story, and this, because of its heavy crust of English gentility and American pseudogentility, was pretty hard to get moving.

I doubt that Hammett had any deliberate artistic aims whatever; he was trying to make a living by writing something he had firsthand information about. He made some of it up; all writers do; but it had a basis in fact; it was made up out of real things. The only reality the English detection writers knew was the conversational accent of Surbiton and Bognor Regis. If they wrote about dukes and Venetian vases, they knew no more about them out of their own experience than the well-heeled Hollywood character knows about the French Modernists that hang in his Bel-Air château or the semi-antique Chippendale-cum-cobbler's bench that he uses for a coffee table. Hammett took murder out of the Venetian vase and dropped it into the alley; it doesn't have to stay there forever, but it looked like a good idea to get as far as possible from Emily Post's idea of how a well-bred débutante gnaws a chicken wing.

Hammett wrote at first (and almost to the end) for people with a sharp, aggressive attitude to life. They were not afraid of the seamy side of things; they lived there. Violence did not dismay them; it was right down their street. Hammett gave murder back to the kind of people that commit it for reasons, not just to provide a corpse; and with the means at hand, not hand-wrought dueling pistols, curare and tropical fish. He put these people down on paper as they were, and he made them talk and think in the language they customarily used for these purposes.

He had style, but his audience didn't know it, because it was in a language not supposed to be capable of such refinements. They thought they were getting a good meaty melodrama written in the kind of lingo they imagined they spoke themselves. It was, in a sense, but it was much more. All language begins with speech, and the speech of common men at that, but when it develops to the point of becoming a literary medium it only looks like speech. Hammett's style at its worst was as formalized as a page of *Marius the Epicurean;* at its best it could say almost anything. I believe this style, which does not belong to Hammett or to anybody, but is the American language (and not even exclusively that any more), can say things he did not know how to say, or feel the need of saying. In his hands it had no overtones, left no echo, evoked no image beyond a distant hill.

Hammett is said to have lacked heart; yet the story he himself thought the most of is the record of a man's devotion to a friend. He was spare, frugal, hard-boiled, but he did over and over again what only the best writers can ever do at all. He wrote scenes that seemed never to have been written before.

With all this he did not wreck the formal detective story. Nobody can; production demands a form that can be produced. Realism takes too much talent, too much knowledge, too much awareness. Hammett may have loosened it up a little here, and sharpened it a little there. Certainly all but the stupidest and most meretricious writers are more conscious of their artificiality than they used to be. And he demonstrated that the detective story can be important writing. *The Maltese Falcon* may or may not be a work of genius, but an art which is capable of it is not "by hypothesis" incapable of anything. Once a detective story can be as good as this, only the pedants will deny that it *could* be even better.

Hammett did something else; he made the detective story fun to write, not an exhausting concatenation of insignificant clues. Without him there might not have been a regional mystery as clever as Percival Wilde's *Inquest,* or an ironic study as able as Raymond Postgate's *Verdict of Twelve,* or a savage piece of intellectual double-talk like Kenneth Fearing's *The Dagger of the Mind,* or a tragi-comic idealization of the murderer as in Donald Henderson's *Mr. Bowling Buys a Newspaper,* or even a gay Hollywoodian gambol like Richard Sale's *Lazarus No. 7.*

The realistic style is easy to abuse: from haste, from lack of awareness, from inability to bridge the chasm that lies between what a writer would like to be able to say and what he actually knows how to say. It is easy to fake; brutality is not strength, flipness is not wit, edge-of-the-chair writing can be as boring as flat writing; dalliance with promiscuous blondes can be very dull stuff when described by goaty young men with no other purpose in mind than to describe dalliance with promiscuous blondes. There has been so much of this sort of thing that if a character in a detective story says "Yeah," the author is automatically a Hammett imitator.

And there are still a number of people around who say that Hammett did not write detective stories at all—merely hard-boiled chronicles of mean streets with a perfunctory mystery element dropped in like the olive in a martini. There are the flustered old ladies—of both sexes (or no sex) and almost all ages—who like their murders scented with magnolia blossoms and do not care to be reminded that murder is an act of infinite cruelty, even if the perpetrators sometimes look like playboys or college professors or nice motherly women with softly graying hair.

There are also a few badly scared champions of the formal or classic mystery who think that no story is a detective story which does not pose a formal and exact problem and arrange the clues around it with neat labels on them. Such would point out, for example, that in reading *The Maltese Falcon* no one concerns himself with who killed Spade's partner, Archer (which is the only formal problem of the story), because the reader is kept thinking about something else. Yet in *The Glass Key* the reader is constantly reminded that the question is who killed Taylor Henry, and exactly the same effect is obtained—an effect of movement, intrigue, cross-purposes, and the gradual elucidation of character, which is all the detective story has any right to be about anyway. The rest is spillikins in the parlor.

But all this (and Hammett too) is for me not quite enough. The realist in murder writes of a world in which gangsters can rule nations and almost rule cities, in which hotels and apartment houses and celebrated restaurants are owned by men who made their money out of brothels, in which a screen star can be the finger man for a mob, and the nice man down the hall is a boss of the numbers racket; a world where a judge with a cellar full of bootleg liquor can send a man to jail for having a pint in his pocket, where the mayor of your town may have condoned murder as an instrument of money-making, where no man can walk down a dark street in safety because law and order are things we talk about but refrain from practicing; a world where you may witness a holdup in broad daylight and see who did it, but you will fade quickly back into the crowd rather than tell anyone, because the holdup men may have friends with long guns, or the police may not like your testimony, and in any case the shyster for the defense will be allowed to abuse and vilify you in open court, before a jury of selected morons, without any but the most perfunctory interference from a political judge.

It is not a fragrant world, but it is the world you live in, and certain writers with tough minds and a cool spirit of detachment can make very interesting and even amusing patterns out of it. It is not funny that a man should be killed, but it is sometimes funny that he should be killed for so little, and that his death should be the coin of what we call civilization. All this still is not quite enough.

In everything that can be called art there is a quality of redemption. It may be pure tragedy, if it is high tragedy, and it may be pity and irony, and it may be the raucous laughter of the strong man. But down these mean streets a man must go who is not himself mean, who is neither tarnished nor afraid. The detective in this kind of story must be such a man. He is the hero; he is everything. He must be a complete man and a common man and yet an unusual man. He must be, to use a rather weathered phrase, a man of honor—by instinct, by inevitability, without thought of it, and certainly without saying it. He must be the best man in his world and a good enough man for any world. I do not care much about his private life; he is neither a eunuch nor a satyr; I think he might seduce a duchess and I am quite sure he would not spoil a virgin; if he is a man of honor in one thing, he is that in all things.

He is a relatively poor man, or he would not be a detective at all. He is a common man or he could not go among common people. He has a sense of character, or he would not know his job. He will take no man's money dishonestly and no man's insolence without a due and dispassionate revenge. He is a lonely man and his pride is that you will treat him as a proud man or be very sorry you ever saw him. He talks as the man of his age talks—that is, with rude wit, a lively sense of the grotesque, a disgust for sham, and a contempt for pettiness.

The story is this man's adventure in search of a hidden truth, and it would be no adventure if it did not happen to a man fit for adventure. He has a range of awareness that startles you, but it belongs to him by right, because it belongs to the world he lives in. If there were enough like him, the world would be a very safe place to live in, without becoming too dull to be worth living in.

(1950)

EUDORA WELTY (1909–2001)

"WORDS INTO FICTION"

Eudora Welty was born in 1909 in Jackson, Mississippi—the city that later provided the inspiration for much of her fiction. Welty began writing in earnest while working as a photographer for the Works Progress Administration, traveling in the Deep South to record scenes of rural life. Her first short story, "Death of a Traveling Salesman," was published in 1936, followed five years later by her first collection of stories, *A Curtain of Green*. Although she earned her reputation primarily as a short story writer, it was for her novel *The Optimist's Daughter* that Eudora Welty was awarded the 1973 Pulitzer Prize.

In "Words into Fiction" Eudora Welty explores what it is that fiction is made of. Although the title may suggest that fiction is comprised simply of words, this essay goes far beyond an examination of language to focus on the feelings, subjects, moments, and mysteries in life that are the real substance of story.

We start from scratch, and words don't; which is the thing that matters—matters over and over again. For though we grow up in the language, when we begin using words to make a piece of fiction, that is of course as different from using even the same words to say hello on the telephone as putting paint on canvas is. This very leap in the dark is exactly what writers write fiction in order to try. And surely they discovered that daring, and developed that wish, from reading. My feeling is that it's when reading begins to impress on us what degrees and degrees and degrees of communication are possible between novelists and ourselves as readers that we surmise what it has meant, can mean, to write novels.

Indeed, learning to write may be a part of learning to read. For all I know, writing comes out of a superior devotion to reading. I feel sure that serious writing does come, must come, out of devotion to the thing itself, to fiction as an art. Both reading and writing are experiences—lifelong—in the course of which we who encounter words used in certain ways are persuaded by them to be brought mind and heart within the presence, the power, of the imagination. This we find to be above all the power to reveal, with nothing barred.

But of course writing fiction, which comes out of life and has the object of showing it, can't be learned from copying out of books. Imitation, or what is in any respect secondhand, is precisely what writing is not. How it is learned can only remain in general—like all else that is personal—an open question; and if ever it's called settled, or solved, the day of fiction is already over. The solution will be the last rites at the funeral. Only the writing of fiction keeps fiction alive. Regardless of whether or not it is reading that gives writing birth, a society that no longer writes novels is not very likely to read any novels at all.

Since we must and do write each our own way, we may during actual writing get more lasting instruction not from another's work, whatever its blessings, however better it is than ours, but from our own poor scratched-over pages. For these we can hold up to life. That is, we are born with a mind and heart to hold each page up to, and to ask: is it valid?

Reading the work of other writers and in the whole, and our long thoughts in retrospect, can tell us all we are able to know of fiction and at firsthand, but this is about *reading*.

The writer himself studies intensely how to do it while he is in the thick of doing it; then when the particular novel or story is done, he is likely to forget how; he does well to. Each work is new. Mercifully, the question of *how* abides less in the abstract, and less in the past, than in the specific, in the work at hand; I chance saying this is so with most writers. Maybe some particular problems, with their confusions and might-have-beens, could be seen into with profit just at the windup, but more likely it's already too late. Already the *working* insight, which is what counts, is gone—along with the story it made, that made it.

And rightly. Fiction finished has to bear the responsibility of its own meaning, it is its own memory. It is now a thing apart from the writer; like a letter mailed, it is nearer by now to its reader. If the writer has had luck, it has something of its own to travel on, something that can make it persist for a while, an identity, before it must fade.

How can I express outside fiction what I think this reality of fiction is?

As a child I was led, an unwilling sightseer, into Mammoth Cave in Kentucky, and after our party had been halted in the blackest hole yet and our guide had let us wait guessing in cold dark what would happen to us, suddenly a light was struck. And we stood in a prism. The chamber was bathed in color, and there was nothing else, we and our guide alike were blotted out by radiance. As I remember, nobody said boo. Gradually we could make out that there was a river in the floor, black as night, which appeared to come out of a closet in the wall; and then, on it, a common rowboat, with ordinary countrified people like our-selves sitting in it, mute, wearing hats, came floating out and on by, and exited into the closet in the opposite wall. I suppose they were simply a party taking the more expensive tour. As we tourists mutually and silently stared, our guide treated us to a recitation on bats, how they lived in uncounted numbers down here and reached light by shooting up winding mile-high chim-neys through rock, never touching by so much as the crook of a wing. He had memorized the speech, and we didn't see a bat. Then the light was put out—just as it is after you've had your two cents' worth in the Baptistry of Florence, where of course more happens: the thing I'm trying here to leave out. As again we stood damp and cold and not able to see our feet, while we each now had something of our own out of it, presumably, what I for one remember is how right I had been in telling my par-ents it would be a bore. For I was too ignorant to know there might be more, or even less, in there than I could see unaided.

Fiction is not the cave; and human life, fiction's territory, merely contains caves. I am only trying to express what I think the so-called raw material is *without its interpretation;* without its artist. Without the act of human understanding—and it is a double act through which we make sense to each other—expe-rience is the worst kind of emptiness; it is obliteration, black or prismatic, as meaningless as was indeed that loveless cave.

Before there is meaning, there has to occur some personal act of vision. And it is this that is continuously projected as the novelist writes, and again as we, each to ourselves, read.

If this makes fiction sound full of mystery, I think it's fuller than I know how to say. Plot, characters, setting, and so forth, are not what I'm referring to now; we all deal with those as best we can. The mystery lies in the use of language to express human life.

In writing, do we try to solve this mystery? No, I think we take hold of the other end of the stick. In very practical ways, we rediscover the mystery. We even, I might say, take advantage of it.

As we know, a body of criticism stands ready to provide its solution, which is a kind of translation of fiction into another language. It offers us close analysis, like a headphone we can clamp on at the U.N. When they are speaking the Arabian tongue. I feel that we can accept this but only with distinct reservations—not about its brilliance or its worth, but about its time and place of application. While we are in the middle of reading some novel, the possibility of the critical phrase "in other words" is one to destroy, rather than make for, a real—that is, imaginative—understanding of the author. Indeed, it is one sure way to break off his carefully laid connection.

Fiction is made to show forth human life, in some chosen part and aspect. A year or so of one writer's life has gone into the writing of a novel, and then to the reader—so long at least as he is reading it—it may be something in his life. There is a remarkable chance of give-and-take. Does this not suggest that, in the novel at least, words have been found for which there may be no other words? If fiction matters—and many lives are at stake that it does—there can be, for the duration of the book, *no* other words.

The point for us if we write is that nearly everything we can learn about writing can be set down only in fiction's terms. What we know about writing the novel *is* the novel.

Try to tear it down, take it back to its beginning, and you are not so much lost as simply nowhere. Some things once done you can't undo, and I hope and believe fiction is one of them. What

its own author knows about a novel is flexible till the end; it
changes as it goes, and more than that, it will not be the same
knowledge he has by the time the work ends as he had when it
began. There is a difference not so much in measure of knowledge, which you would take for granted, as in kind of knowledge. The idea is now the object. The idea is something that you
or I might just conceivably have had in common with the author,
in the vague free air of the everyday. But not by the wildest
chance should we be able to duplicate by one sentence what
happened to the idea; neither could the author himself write the
same novel again. As he works, his own revision, even though he
throws away his changes, can never be wholly undone. The
novel has passed through that station on its track. And as readers, we too proceed by the author's arbitrary direction to his
one-time-only destination: a journey rather strange, hardly in a
straight line, altogether personal.

There has occurred the experience of the writer in writing the
novel, and now there occurs the experience of the reader in
reading it. More than one mind and heart go into this. We may
even hope to follow into a kind of future with a novel that to us
seems good, drawn forward by what the long unfolding has
promised and so far revealed. By yielding to what has been, by
all his available means, *suggested*, we are able to see for ourselves a certain distance beyond what is possible for him simply
to *say*. So that, although nobody else ought to say this, the novelist *has* said, "In other words . . ."

Thus all fiction may be seen as a symbol, if this is desired—
and how often it is, so it seems. But surely the novel exists within the big symbol of fiction itself—not the other way round, as a
conglomeration of little symbols. I think that fiction is the hen,
not the egg, and that the good live hen came first.

Certainly symbols fill our daily lives, our busily communicative, if not always communicating, world; and any number of
them come with perfect naturalness into our daily conversation
and our behavior. And they are a legitimate part of fiction, as
they have always been of every art—desirable as any device is,
so long as it serves art. Symbols have to spring from the work

direct, and stay alive. Symbols for the sake of symbols are coun-
terfeit, and were they all stamped on the page in red they
couldn't any more quickly give themselves away. So are symbols
failing their purpose when they don't keep to proportion in the
book. However alive they are, they should never call for an
emphasis greater than the emotional reality they serve, in their
moment, to illuminate. One way of looking at Moby Dick is that
his task as a symbol was so big and strenuous that he *had* to be
a whale.

Most symbols that a fiction writer uses, however carefully,
today are apt to be as swiftly spotted by his reader as the smoke
signals that once crossed our plains from Indian to Indian. Using
symbols and—still worse—finding symbols is such a habit. It
follows that too little comes to be suggested, and this, as can
never be affirmed often enough, is the purpose of every word
that goes into a piece of fiction. The imagination has to be
involved, and more—ignited.

How much brighter than the symbol can be the explicit
observation that springs firsthand from deep and present feeling
in one breast. Indeed, it is something like this, spontaneous in
effect, pure in effect, that takes on the emotional value of a symbol when it was first minted, but which as time passes shrinks to
become only a counter.

When Chekhov says there were so many stars out that one
could not have put a finger between them, he gives us more
than night, he gives us *that* night. For symbols can only grow to
be the same when the same experiences on which fiction is
based are more and more partaken of by us all. But Chekhov's
stars, some as large as a goose's egg and some as small as
hempseed, are still exactly where they were, in the sky of his
story "Easter Eve." And from them to us that night still travels—
for so much more than symbols, they are Chekhov looking at his
sky.

Communication through fiction frequently happens, I
believe, in ways that are small—a word is not too small; that are
unannounced; that are less direct than we might first suppose
on seeing how important they are. It isn't communication hap-
pening when you as the reader follow or predict the novel's plot

or agree with, or anticipate, or could even quote the characters; when you hail the symbols; even when its whole landscape and climate have picked you up and transported you where it happens. But communication is going on, and regardless of all the rest, when you believe the writer.

Then is plausibility at the bottom of it? When we can read and say, "Oh, how right, I think so too," has the writer come through? Only stop to think how often simple plausibility, if put to measure a good story, falls down, while the story stands up, never wavers. And agreement isn't always, by any means, a mark of having been reached.

As a reader who never held a gun, I risk saying that it isn't exactly plausible that Old Ben, the bear in Faulkner's story, when he was finally brought down by a knife-thrust, had already in him fifty-two little hard lumps which were old bullets that had had no effect on him. Yet as a reader caught in the story, I think I qualify to bear witness that nothing less than fifty-two bullets could have been embedded in Old Ben or Old Ben he would not be. Old Ben and every one of his bullets along with him are parts of the truth in this story, William Faulkner's particular truth.

Belief doesn't depend on plausibility, but it seems to be a fact that validity of a kind, and this is of course a subjective kind, gained in whatever way that had to be, is the quality that makes a work reliable as art. This reliability comes straight out of the writer himself. In the end, it is another personal quotient in writing fiction; it is something inimitable. It is that by which each writer *lets us believe*—doesn't ask us to, can't make us, simply lets us.

To a large extent a writer cannot help the material of his fiction. That is, he cannot help where and when he happened to be born; then he has to live somewhere and somehow and with others, and survive through some history or other if he is here to write at all. But it is not to escape his life but more to pin it down that he writes fiction (though by pinning it down he no doubt does escape it a little). And so certainly he does choose his subject. It's not really quibbling to say that a writer's subject, in due time, chooses the writer—not of course *as* a writer, but as the

man or woman who comes across it by living and has it to struggle with. That person may come on it by seeming accident, like
falling over a chair in a dark room. But he may invite it with
wide-open arms, so that it eventually walks in. Or his subject
may accrue, build up and build up inside him until it's intolerable to him not to try to write it in terms he can understand: he
submits it to the imagination, he finds names, sets something
down. "In other words . . ."

So he does choose his subject, though not without compulsion, and now not too much stands in the way of the writer's
learning something for himself about his own writing. For he
has taken the fatal step when he put himself into his subject's
hands. He might even do well to feel some misgivings: he and
his fiction were never strangers, but at moments he may wonder
at the ruthlessness of the relationship, which is honesty,
between it and himself.

His inspiration, so-called, may very easily, then, be personal
desperation—painful or pleasurable. All kinds of desperation
get to be one in the work. But it will be the particular desperation that the particular writer is heir to, subject to, out of which
he learns in daily life, by which, in that year, he is driven, on
which he can feel, think, construct something, write out in as
many drafts as he likes and then not get to much of an end.
What he checks his work against remains, all the way, not books,
not lore, neither another's writing nor in the large his own, but
life that breathes in his face. Still he may get to *his* end, have *his*
say.

It really is his say. We have the writer's own vision of everything in the world when we place his novel in the center. Then
so much is clear: how he sees life and death, how much he
thinks people matter to each other and to themselves, how
much he would like you to know what he finds beautiful or
strange or awful or absurd, what he can do without, how well he
has learned to see, hear, touch, smell—all as his sentences go by
and in their time and sequence mount up. It grows clear how he
imposes order and structure on his fictional world; and it is ter-
ribly clear, in the end, whether, when he calls for understanding,
he gets any.

And of course he knew this would be so: he has been, and he is, a *reader*. Furthermore, all his past is in his point of view; his novel, whatever its subject, is the history itself of his life's experience in feeling. He has invited us, while we are his readers, to see with his point of view. Can we see? And what does he feel passionately about? Is it honest passion? The answer to that we know from the opening page. For some reason, honesty is one thing that it's almost impossible to make a mistake about in reading fiction.

Let us not think, however, that we ever plumb it all—not one whole novel; and I am not speaking of the great ones exclusively. It is for quite other reasons that we never know all of a single person. But the finished novel transcends the personal in art. Indeed, that has been its end in view.

For fiction, ideally, is highly personal but objective. It is something which only you can write but which is not, necessarily, *about* you. Style, I think, is whatever it is in the prose which has constantly pressed to give the writing its objectivity. Style does not obtrude but exists as the sum total of all the ways that have been taken to make the work stand on its own, apart. Born subjective, we learn what our own idea of the objective is as we go along.

Style is a product of highly conscious effort but is not self-conscious. Even with esthetic reasons aside, the self-consciousness would not be justified. For if you have worked in any serious way, you *have* your style—like the smoke from a fired cannon, like the ring in the water after the fish is pulled out or jumps back in. I can't see that a writer deserves praise in particular for his style, however good: in order for him to have written what he must have very much wanted to write, a way had to be found. A reader's understanding of his style—as the picture, or the reflection, or the proof of a way in which communication tried to happen—is more to be wished for than any praise; and when communication does happen, the style is in effect beyond praise.

What you write about is in the public domain. Subject you can choose, but your mind and heart compel you. Point of view you develop in order to transcend it. Style you acquire in the pursuit of something else which may turn out to be the impossible. Now let me mention shape.

In fiction, as we know, the shapes the work takes are marvelous, and vary most marvelously in our minds. It is hard to speak further about them. Specific in the work, in the mind, but not describable anywhere else—or not by me; shape is something felt. It is the form of the work that you feel to be under way as you write and as you read. At the end, instead of farewell, it tells over the whole, as a whole, to the reader's memory.

In sculpture, this shape is left in rock itself and stands self-identifying and self-announcing. Fiction is made of words to travel under the reading eye, and made to go in one sequence and one direction, slowly, accumulating; time is an element. The words follow the contours of some continuous relationship between what can be told and what cannot be told, to be in the silence of reading the lightest of the hammers that tap their way along this side of chaos.

Fiction's progress is of course not tactile, though at once you might rejoin by saying that some of Lawrence's stories, for instance, *are*—as much as a stroke of the hand down a horse's neck. Neither is shape necessarily, or even often, formal, though James, for example, was so fond of making it so. There is no more limit to the kinds of shape a fictional work may take than there appears to be to the range and character of our minds.

The novel or story ended, shape must have made its own impression on the reader, so that he feels that some design in life (by which I mean esthetic pattern, not purpose) has just been discovered there. And this pattern, shape, form that emerges for you then, a reader at the end of the book, may do the greatest thing that fiction does: it may move you. And however you have been moved by the parts, this still has to happen from the whole before you know what indeed you have met with in that book.

From the writer's view, we might say that shape is most closely connected with the work itself, is the course it ran. From the reader's view, we might say that shape is connected with recognition; it is what allows us to know and remember what in the world of feeling we have been living through in that novel. The part of the mind in both reader and writer that form speaks to may be the deep-seated perception we all carry in us of the beauty of order imposed, of structure rising and building upon itself, and finally of this coming to rest.

It is through the shaping of the work in the hands of the artist that you most nearly come to know what can be known, on the page, of his mind and heart, and his as apart from the others. No other saw life in an ordering exactly like this. So shape begins and ends subjectively. And that the two concepts, writer's and reader's, may differ, since all of us differ, is neither so strange nor so important as the vital fact that a connection has been made between them. Our whole reading lives testify to the astonishing degree to which this can happen.

This ordering, or shape, a felt thing that emerges whole for us at the very last, as we close the novel to think back, was to the writer, I think, known first thing of all. It was surmised. And this is above all what nobody else knew or could have taught or told him. Besides, at that point he was not their listener. He could not, it seems, have cast his work except in the mold it's in, which was there in his mind all the hard way through. And this notwithstanding thousands of other things that life crowded into his head, parts of the characters that we shall never meet, flashes of action that yielded to other flashes, conversations drowned out, pieces of days and nights, all to be given up, and rightly.

For we have to remember what the novel is. Made by the imagination for the imagination, it is an illusion come full circle—a very exclusive thing, for all it seems to include a good deal of the world. It was wholly for the sake of illusion, made by art out of, and in order to show, and to be, some human truth, that the novelist took all he knew with him and made that leap in the dark.

For he must already have apprehended and come to his own jumping-off place before he could put down on paper that ever-miraculous thing, the opening sentence.

(1965)

KURT VONNEGUT (b. 1922)

"HOW TO WRITE WITH STYLE"

Kurt Vonnegut, Jr. was born in Indianapolis, Indiana in 1922. As a soldier in the U.S. Air Force during World War II, he was captured by the Germans and witnessed the infamous firebombing of Dresden. His experiences as a prisoner of war influenced much of his work, especially *Slaughterhouse Five*—arguably Vonnegut's finest and most important novel. Although his later works are known for their satirical experimentalism, Vonnegut began his career primarily as a science fiction writer, with such novels as *Player Piano* (1952) and *Cat's Cradle* (1963). Upon the publication of the semi-autobiographical novel *Timequake* in 1997, Kurt Vonnegut announced his retirement from fiction. He now lives and writes nonfiction in his eastside townhouse in New York City.

In this brief essay, characterized by the author's signature wit and charm, Vonnegut offers the reader valuable advice on the matter of style. Instead of preaching about the villainy of adverbs and passive sentences, as one might expect, he discusses the subjects that writers choose to write about, and how they can make them come alive through artful language.

Newspaper reporters and technical writers are trained to reveal almost nothing about themselves in their writings. This makes them freaks in the world of writers, since almost all of the other ink-stained wretches in that world reveal a lot about themselves to readers. We call these revelations, accidental and intentional, elements of literary style.

These revelations are fascinating to us as readers. They tell us what sort of person it is with whom we are spending time. Does the writer sound ignorant or informed, crazy or sane, stupid or bright, crooked or honest, humorless or playful—? And on and on.

When you yourself put words on paper, remember that the most damning revelation you can make about yourself is that you do not know what is interesting and what is not. Don't you yourself like or dislike writers mainly for what they choose to show you or make you think about? Did you ever admire an empty-headed writer for his or her mastery of the language? No.

So your own winning literary style must begin with interesting ideas in your head. Find a subject you care about and which you in your heart feel others should care about. It is this genuine caring, and not your games with language, which will be the most compelling and seductive element in your style.

I am not urging you to write a novel, by the way—although I would not be sorry if you wrote one, provided you genuinely cared about something. A petition to the mayor about a pothole in front of your house or a love letter to the girl next door will do.

Do not ramble, though.

As for your use of language: Remember that two great masters of our language, William Shakespeare and James Joyce, wrote sentences which were almost childlike when their subjects were most profound. "To be or not to be?" asks Shakespeare's Hamlet. The longest word is three letters long. Joyce, when he was frisky, could put together a sentence as intricate and glittering as a necklace for Cleopatra, but my favorite sentence in his short story "Eveline" is this one: "She was tired." At that point in the story, no other words could break the heart of a reader as those words do.

Simplicity of language is not only reputable, but perhaps even sacred. The Bible opens with a sentence well within the writing skills of a lively fourteen-year-old: "In the beginning God created the heavens and the earth."

It may be that you, too, are capable of making necklaces for Cleopatra, so to speak. But your eloquence should be the servant of the ideas in your head. Your rule might be this: If a sentence, no matter how excellent, does not illuminate my subject in some new and useful way, scratch it out. Here is the same rule paraphrased to apply to storytelling, to fiction: Never include a sentence which does not either remark on character or advance the action.

The writing style which is most natural for you is bound to echo speech you heard when a child. English was the novelist Joseph Conrad's third language, and much that seems piquant in his use of English was no doubt colored by his first language, which was Polish. And lucky indeed is the writer who has grown up in Ireland, for the English spoken there is so amusing and musical. I myself grew up in Indianapolis, Indiana, where common speech sounds like a band saw cutting galvanized tin, and employs a vocabulary as unornamental as a monkey wrench.

In some of the more remote hollows of Appalachia, children still grow up hearing songs and locutions of Elizabethan times. Yes, and many Americans grow up hearing a language other than English, or an English dialect a majority of Americans cannot understand.

All these varieties of speech are beautiful, just as the varieties of butterflies are beautiful. No matter what your first language, you should treasure it all your life. If it happens not to be standard English, and if it shows itself when you write standard English, the result is usually delightful, like a very pretty girl with one eye that is green and one that is blue.

I myself find that I trust my own writing most, and others seem to trust it most, too, when I sound most like a person from Indianapolis, which is what I am. What alternatives do I have? The one most vehemently recommended by teachers has no doubt been pressed on you, as well: that I write like cultivated Englishmen of a century or more ago.

I used to be exasperated by such teachers, but am no more. I understand now that all those antique essays and stories with which I was to compare my own work were not magnificent for their datedness or foreignness, but for saying precisely what their authors meant them to say. My teachers wished me to write accurately, always selecting the most effective words, and relating the words to one another unambiguously, rigidly, like parts of a machine. The teachers did not want to turn me into an Englishman after all. They hoped that I would become understandable—and therefore understood.

And there went my dream of doing with words what Pablo Picasso did with paint or what any number of jazz idols did with music. If I broke all the rules of punctuation, had words mean whatever I wanted them to mean, and strung them together higgledy-piggledy, I would simply not be understood. So you, too, had better avoid Picasso-style or jazz-style writing, if you have something worth saying and wish to be understood.

If it were only teachers who insisted that modern writers stay close to literary styles of the past, we might reasonably ignore them. But readers insist on the very same thing. They want our pages to look very much like pages they have seen before.

Why? It is because they themselves have a tough job to do, and they need all the help they can get from us. They have to identify thousands of little marks on paper, and make sense of them immediately. They have to *read,* an art so difficult that most people do not really master it even after having studied it all through grade school and high school—for twelve long years.

So this discussion, like all discussions of literary styles, must finally acknowledge that our stylistic options as writers are neither numerous nor glamorous, since our readers are bound to be such imperfect artists. Our audience requires us to be sympathetic and patient teachers, ever willing to simplify and clarify—whereas we would rather soar high above the crowd, singing like nightingales.

That is the bad news. The good news is that we Americans are governed under a unique Constitution, which allows us to write whatever we please without fear of punishment. So the most meaningful aspect of our styles, which is what we choose to write about, is unlimited.

Also: we are members of an egalitarian society, so there is no reason for us to write, in case we are not classically educated aristocrats, as though we were classically educated aristocrats.

For a discussion of literary style in a narrower sense, in a more technical sense, commend to your attention *The Elements of Style* by William Strunk, Jr., and E. B. White (Macmillan, 1979). It contains such rules as this: "A participial phrase at the beginning of a sentence must refer to the grammatical subject," and so on. E. B. White is, of course, one of the most admirable literary stylists this country has so far produced.

You should realize, too, that no one would care how well or badly Mr. White expressed himself, if he did not have perfectly enchanting things to say.

(1980)

RAYMOND CARVER (1938–1988)

"ON WRITING"

Born in Clatskanie, Oregon in 1938 and raised in Yakima, Washington, Raymond Carver married his girlfriend, Maryann Burk, one year after graduating from high school. He went on to work as a janitor, gas-station attendant, and delivery boy before he became seriously interested in fiction. Carver began writing in 1958 while taking a course on the subject at Chico State College, although he did not have any real literary success until the 1967 publication of his short story, "Will You Please Be Quiet, Please?" He followed this effort with the critically acclaimed collection of the same name in 1970. Carver published his second major collection in 1981, *What We Talk About When We Talk About Love;* and in 1983 received the lucrative Mildred and Harold Strauss Living Award, which allowed him to devote the rest of his life solely to writing. Soon after, he published two of his greatest short story collections: *Cathedral* (1984), and *Where I'm Calling From* (1988). Raymond Carver died from lung cancer at the age of 50 in 1988—the same year he was inducted into the American Academy of Arts and Letters.

The following is a bit of a rambling meditation on all things related to the art and craft of fiction. In it, Carver discusses his likes and dislikes as a reader, his process as a writer, and his philosophies as an artist. In every paragraph—whether it be on criticism or craft—the reader will find useful guidance conveyed by the inspiring voice of firsthand experience.

Back in the mid-1960s, I found I was having trouble concentrating my attention on long narrative fiction. For a time I experienced difficulty in trying to read it as well as in attempting to write it. My attention span had gone out on me; I no longer had the patience to try to write novels. It's an involved story, too tedious to talk about here. But I know it has much to do now with why I write poems and short stories. Get in, get out. Don't linger. Go on. It could be that I lost any great ambitions at about the same time, in my late twenties. If I did, I think it was good it happened. Ambition and a little luck are good things for a writer to have going for him. Too much ambition and bad luck, or no luck at all, can be killing. There has to be talent.

Some writers have a bunch of talent; I don't know any writers who are without it. But a unique and exact way of looking at things, and finding the right context for expressing that way of looking, that's something else. *The World According to Garp* is, of course, the marvelous world according to John Irving. There is another world according to Flannery O'Connor, and others according to William Faulkner and Ernest Hemingway. There are worlds according to Cheever, Updike, Singer, Stanley Elkin, Ann Beattie, Cynthia Ozick, Donald Barthelme, Mary Robison, William Kittredge, Barry Hannah, Ursula K. LeGuin. Every great or even every very good writer makes the world over according to his own specifications.

It's akin to style, what I'm talking about, but it isn't style alone. It is the writer's particular and unmistakable signature on everything he writes. It is his world and no other. This is one of the things that distinguishes one writer from another. Not talent. There's plenty of that around. But a writer who has some special way of looking at things and who gives artistic expression to that way of looking: that writer may be around for a time.

Isak Dinesen said that she wrote a little every day, without hope and without despair. Someday I'll put that on a three-by-five card and tape it to the wall beside my desk. I have some three-by-five cards on the wall now. "Fundamental accuracy of statement is the ONE sole morality of writing." Ezra Pound. It is not everything by ANY means, but if a writer has "fundamental accuracy of statement" going for him, he's at least on the right track.

I have a three-by-five up there with this fragment of a sentence from a story by Chekhov: ". . . and suddenly everything became clear to him." I find these words filled with wonder and possibility. I love their simple clarity, and the hint of revelation that's implied. There is mystery, too. What has been unclear before? Why is it just now becoming clear? What's happened?

Most of all—what now? There are consequences as a result of such sudden awakenings. I feel a sharp sense of relief—and anticipation.

I overheard the writer Geoffrey Wolff say "No cheap tricks" to a group of writing students. That should go on a three-by-five card. I'd amend it a little to "No tricks." Period. I hate tricks. At the first sign of a trick or a gimmick in a piece of fiction, a cheap trick or even an elaborate trick, I tend to look for cover. Tricks are ultimately boring, and I get bored easily, which may go along with my not having much of an attention span. But extremely clever chi-chi writing, or just plain tomfoolery writing, puts me to sleep. Writers don't need tricks or gimmicks or even necessarily need to be the smartest fellows on the block. At the risk of appearing foolish, a writer sometimes needs to be able to just stand and gape at this or that thing—a sunset or an old shoe—in absolute and simple amazement.

Some months back, in the *New York Times Book Review*, John Barth said that ten years ago most of the students in his fiction writing seminar were interested in "formal innovation," and this no longer seems to be the case. He's a little worried that writers are going to start writing mom and pop novels in the 1980s. He worries that experimentation may be on the way out, along with liberalism. I get a little nervous if I find myself within earshot of somber discussions about "formal innovation" in fiction writing. Too often "experimentation" is a license to be careless, silly or imitative in the writing. Even worse, a license to try to brutalize or alienate the reader. Too often such writing gives us no news of the world, or else describes a desert landscape and that's all—a few dunes and lizards here and there, but no people; a place uninhabited by anything recognizably human, a place of interest only to a few scientific specialists.

It should be noted that real experiment in fiction is original, hard-earned and cause for rejoicing. But someone else's way of looking at things—Barthelme's, for instance—should not be chased after by other writers. It won't work. There is only one Barthelme, and for another writer to try to appropriate Barthelme's peculiar sensibility or *mise en scene* under the rubric of innovation is for that writer to mess around with chaos and disaster and, worse, self-deception. The real experimenters have to Make It New, as Pound urged, and in the process have to find things out for themselves. But if writers haven't taken leave of their senses, they also want to stay in touch with us, they want to carry news from their world to ours.

It's possible, in a poem or a short story, to write about commonplace things and objects using commonplace but precise language, and to endow those things—a chair, a window curtain, a fork, a stone, a woman's earring—with immense, even startling power. It is possible to write a line of seemingly innocuous dialogue and have it send a chill along the reader's spine—the source of artistic delight, as Nabokov would have it. That's the kind of writing that most interests me. I hate sloppy or haphazard writing whether it flies under the banner of experimentation or else is just clumsily rendered realism. In Isaac Babel's wonderful short story, "Guy de Maupassant," the narrator has this to say about the writing of fiction: "No iron can pierce the heart with such force as a period put just at the right place." This too ought to go on a three-by-five.

Evan Connell said once that he knew he was finished with a short story when he found himself going through it and taking out commas and then going through the story again and putting commas back in the same places. I like that way of working on something. I respect that kind of care for what is being done. That's all we have, finally, the words, and they had better be the right ones, with the punctuation in the right places so that they can best say what they are meant to say. If the words are heavy with the writer's own unbridled emotions, or if they are imprecise and inaccurate for some other reason—if the words are in any way blurred—the reader's eyes will slide right over them and nothing will be achieved. The reader's own artistic sense will simply not be engaged. Henry James called this sort of hapless writing "weak specification."

I have friends who've told me they had to hurry a book because they needed the money, their editor or their wife was leaning on them or leaving them—something, some apology for the writing not being very good. "It would have been better if I'd taken the time." I was dumbfounded when I heard a novelist friend say this. I still am, if I think about it, which I don't. It's none of my business. But if the writing can't be made as good as it is within us to make it, then why do it? In the end, the satisfaction of having done our best, and the proof of that labor, is the one thing we can take into the grave. I wanted to say to my friend, for heaven's sake go do something else. There have to be easier and maybe more honest ways to try and earn a living. Or else just do it to the best of your abilities, your talents, and then don't justify or make excuses. Don't complain, don't explain.

In an essay called, simply enough, "Writing Short Stories," Flannery O'Connor talks about writing as an act of discovery. O'Connor says she most often did not know where she was going when she sat down to work on a short story. She says she doubts that many writers know where they are going when they begin something. She uses "Good Country People" as an example of how she put together a short story whose ending she could not even guess at until she was nearly there:

When I started writing that story, I didn't know there was going to be a Ph.D. with a wooden leg in it. I merely found myself one morning writing a description of two women I knew something about, and before I realized it, I had equipped one of them with a daughter with a wooden leg. I brought in the Bible salesman, but I had no idea what I was going to do with him. I didn't know he was going to steal that wooden leg until ten or twelve lines before he did it, but when I found out that this was what was going to happen, I realized it was inevitable.

When I read this some years ago it came as a shock that she, or anyone for that matter, wrote stories in this fashion. I thought this was my uncomfortable secret, and I was a little uneasy with it. For sure I thought this way of working on a short story somehow revealed my own shortcomings. I remember being tremendously heartened by reading what she had to say on the subject.

I once sat down to write what turned out to be a pretty good story, though only the first sentence of the story had offered itself to me when I began it. For several days I'd been going around with this sentence in my head: "He was running the vacuum cleaner when the telephone rang." I knew a story was there and that it wanted telling. I felt it in my bones, that a story belonged with that beginning, if I could just have the time to write it. I found the time, an entire day—twelve, fifteen hours even—if I wanted to make use of it. I did, and I sat down in the morning and wrote the first sentence, and other sentences promptly began to attach themselves. I made the story just as I'd make a poem; one line and then the next, and the next. Pretty soon I could see a story, and I knew it was my story, the one I'd been wanting to write.

I like it when there is some feeling of threat or sense of menace in short stories. I think a little menace is fine to have in a story. For one thing, it's good for the circulation. There has to be tension, a sense that something is imminent, that certain things are in relentless motion, or else, most often, there simply won't be a story. What creates tension in a piece of fiction is partly the way the concrete words are linked together to make up the visible action of the story. But it's also the things that are left out, that are implied, the landscape just under the smooth (but sometimes broken and unsettled) surface of things.

V.S. Pritchett's definition of a short story is "something glimpsed from the corner of the eye, in passing." Notice the "glimpse" part of this. First the glimpse. Then the glimpse given life, turned into something that illuminates the moment and may, if we're lucky—that word again—have even further-ranging consequences and meaning. The short story writer's task is to invest the glimpse with all that is in his power. He'll bring his intelligence and literary skill to bear (his talent), his sense of proportion and sense of the fitness of things: of how things out there really are and how he sees those things—like no one else sees them. And this is done through the use of clear and specific language, language used so as to bring to life the details that will light up the story for the reader. For the details to be concrete and convey meaning, the language must be accurate and precisely given. The words can be so precise they may even sound flat, but they can still carry; if used right, they can hit all the notes.

(1981)

WALLACE STEGNER (1909–1993)

"TO A YOUNG WRITER"

Wallace Stegner was born in Lake Mills, Iowa on February 18, 1909. Over the course of his career as a writer and teacher, Stegner wrote over sixty books of fiction and nonfiction, while teaching at the University of Wisconsin, Harvard University, and Stanford University, where he directed the creative writing program. Stegner's fifth novel, *The Big Rock Candy Mountain* (1943), was his first popular success, although it was *Angle of Repose* that won him the Pulitzer Prize for Fiction in 1972, and *The Spectator Bird* that won him the National Book Award in 1977. Wallace Stegner died in 1993 due to injuries sustained from a car accident in Santa Fe, New Mexico.

One of the most heartfelt and touching essays in this collection, this piece is in fact a letter of advice written to a young writer upon the completion of her first novel. Unsparing in its honesty, this essay describes the difficult but necessary road that lies ahead for all new writers.

Your note asks advice on some purely practical matters, and to most of your questions the answers are dead-easy. No, you don't need any agent yet; later you probably will. Yes, you might try lifting sections out of your book and trying them on magazines; it can do no harm, and it might get you an audience or make you some money or both. No, there is no reason why you shouldn't apply for one of the available fellowships: Guggenheim or Saxton or, since you are uncommitted, one of those offered by publishers. By the same token, you are eligible to submit your book to any prize contest and to apply for admission to any of the literary and artistic colonies, such as Yaddo, the MacDowell Colony or the Huntington Hartford Foundation. Even a brief residence in one of these would give you a place to live and write and would remove at least for a few weeks or months the insecurity that has nearly unnerved you. Of course I will write letters to any of these places in your behalf, of course I will give you letters to publishers, and if we happen to be in New York at the same time I will be happy to take you up to an office or two or three and introduce you.

But when I have said this, I am left feeling that most of what you really hoped to hear has been left unsaid. I suspect that much of the reason for your writing me was a need for reassurance: Your confidence had suddenly got gooseflesh and damp palms; you came up out of your book and looked around you and were hit by sudden panic. You would like to be told that you are good and that all this difficulty and struggle and frustration will give way gradually or suddenly, preferably suddenly, to security, fame, confidence, the conviction of having worked well and faithfully to a good end and become someone important to the world. If I am wrong in writing to this unspoken plea, forgive me; it is the sort of thing I felt myself at your age, and still feel, and will never get over feeling.

It is no trouble to tell you that you indeed are good, much too good to remain unpublished. Because publishers are mainly literate and intelligent, most of them are sure to see the quality in your novel, and one of them is sure to publish it. But that is as far as I can honestly go in reassurance, for I suspect he will publish it with little expectation of its making much money, either for him or for you.

Naturally I am not saying anything as foolish as that literary worth and popularity are incompatible. They are proved compatible quite frequently, but almost always when the writer in question possesses some form of the common touch—humor, sentiment, violence, sensationalism, sex, a capacity for alarm— and raises it to the level of art. Shakespeare and Rabelais and Mark Twain didn't exhaust the possibilities of lifting a whole mass of common preoccupations into beauty and significance. But it is your misfortune (and also your specific virtue) to have an uncommon touch. Your virtues are not the virtues of the mass of the population, or even of the reading population. Restraint, repose, compassion, humor that isn't ribald and feeling that isn't sentimental—these are caviar to the general, whatever you and I might wish.

You write better than hundreds of people with established literary reputations. You understand your characters and their implications, and you take the trouble to make sure that they have implications. Without cheating or bellowing or tearing a passion to tatters, you can bring a reader to that alert participation that is the truest proof of fiction's effectiveness. You think ten times where a lot of writers throb once.

And there is very little demand for the cool, perfect things you can do. You have gone threadbare for ten years to discover that your talents are almost sure to go unappreciated.

It is one thing to go threadbare for five or ten years in show business or to spend eight or ten years on a medical or legal education. A man can do it cheerfully, for the jackpots are there in those professions and may be expected by the talented in the course of time. And I suspect that you have had somewhere before you the marshlight of a jackpot, too. After all, every publishing season produces that happy sound of someone's apron being filled with solid, countable money. Your own seven years in college and two and a half years of apprenticeship on this first novel should entitle you to at least the milder sorts of expectation.

Since I participated in it, I know something about your education, and I know that it took. A literary education does not necessarily turn out even a good reader, much less a good writer. But with you it did both. You are a sharpened instrument, ready and willing to be put to work.

For one thing, you never took writing to mean self-expression, which means self-indulgence. You understood from the beginning that writing is done with words and sentences, and you spent hundreds of hours educating your ear, writing and rewriting and rewriting until you began to handle words in combination as naturally as one changes tones with the tongue and lips in whistling. I speak respectfully of this part of your education, because every year I see students who will not submit to it—who have only themselves to say and who are bent upon saying it without concessions to the English language. In acknowledging that the English language is a difficult instrument and that a person who sets out to use it expertly has no alternative but to learn it, you did something else. You forced yourself away from that obsession with self that is the strength of a very few writers and the weakness of so many. You have labored to put yourself in charge of your material; you have not fallen for the romantic fallacy that it is virtue to be driven by it. By submitting to language, you submitted to other disciplines, you learned distance and detachment, you learned how to avoid muddying a story with yourself.

That much the study of writing in college has given you. It might have given you worse things as well, but didn't. It might have made you a coterie writer, might have imprinted on you some borrowed style or some arrogance of literary snobbery, might have made you forever a leaner and a dependent. How many times have I backpedaled from some young man furious to destroy with words the father he thinks he hates; how many times have I turned cold to avoid becoming a surrogate father or even mother. How much compulsive writing have I read, inwardly flinching for the helpless enslavement it revealed. How often the writing of young writers is a way of asserting a personality that isn't yet there, that is only being ravenously hunted for.

None of that in yours. In yours, sanity and light and compassion, not self-love and self-pity. You know who you are, and you are good. Never doubt it—though you could not be blamed if you wistfully wondered. To date, from all your writing, you have made perhaps five hundred dollars, for two short stories and a travel article. To finance school and to write your novel you have lived meagerly with little encouragement and have risked the disapproval of your family, who have understandably said, "Here is this girl nearly thirty years old now, unmarried, without a job or a profession, still mooning away at her writing as if life were forever. Here goes her life through her fingers while she sits in cold rooms and grows stoop-shouldered over a typewriter." So now, with your book finally in hand, you want desperately to have some harvest: a few good reviews, some critical attention, encouragement, royalties enough to let you live and go on writing.

You are entitled to them all, but you may get few or none of them. Some good reviews you undoubtedly will get, but also many routine plus-minus ones that will destroy you with their impercipience, and a few flip ones by bright young men who will patronize you in five hundred words or spend their space telling how trying was the heat on the New Haven as they read this book on the commuters' special. Your initial royalty statement, at an optimistic guess, will indicate that your publisher by hard work built up an advance sale of 2,700 copies. Your next one, six months later, will probably carry the news that 432 of those copies came back and that altogether you fell just a little short of earning the thousand-dollar advance that you spent eight or nine months ago.

All this you are aware of as possibility, because you have the habit of not deceiving yourself and because you have seen it happen to friends. Learn to look upon it as probability.

Having brought yourself to that glum anticipation, ponder your choices. To go on writing as you have been doing—slowly, carefully, with long pauses for thinking and revising—you need some sort of subsidy: fellowship, advance, grant, job, marriage, something. In the nature of things, most of your alternatives will be both temporary and modest. Of the possible jobs, teaching probably offers most, because its hours are flexible and because it entails a three-month summer vacation. You have the training, the degrees, some teaching experience, but for you I would not advise teaching. For one thing, you are so conscientious that you would let it absorb your whole energy. For another, I am sure you can write only if you have full time for it. Your distillation process is slow, drop by drop, and you can't make it produce enough in a few broken weeks of summer. So you will undoubtedly try the fellowships and the colonies, and perhaps for a year or two get by that way.

After that, who knows? You might sell enough to squeak by; you might get a job caring for people's cats while they travel; you might work for a year or two at a time and save enough to take every third year for writing; you might marry. You might even marry and keep on writing, though it often happens otherwise. By the same token, you might find that marriage and children are so adequate a satisfaction of the urges that are driving you to write that you don't need to write, or you may find all the satisfactions of marriage and a family and come back to fiction when your children are grown. You and I both know those who have, and we both know some of the special difficulties they met. However you do it, I imagine you will always be pinched—for money, for time, for a place to work. But I think you will do it. And believe me, it is not a new problem. You are in good company.

Barring marriage, which is an alternative career and not a solution of this one, you may say to yourself that you can't stand such a narrow, gray life, that you will modify your temperament and your taste, and work into your books some of the sensationalism, violence, shock, sentiment, sex, or Great Issues that you think may make them attractive to a large audience. I doubt that you could do it if you wanted to, and I am certain that you shouldn't try, for you cannot write with a whole heart things that are contrary to your nature. The fine things in your first novel are there because you wrote them with a whole heart, from an intense conviction. Trying to write like those who manage a large popular success, you may succeed, because you have brains and skill; but however proper success may be for others, in you, and on these terms, it will not be legitimate, for you will have stopped being the writer that you respected.

You are as whole an instrument as a broom. The brush is no good without the handle, and the whole thing is good only for sweeping. You are scheduled—doomed—to be a serious writer regarding life seriously and reporting it to a small audience. Other kinds of writers are both possible and necessary, but this is the kind you are, and it is a good kind. Not many of your countrymen will read you or know your name, not because they are Americans, or moderns, or especially stupid, but because they are human. Your kind of writer has never spoken to a large audience except over a long stretch of time, and I would not advise you to pin too much hope even on posterity. Your touch is the uncommon touch; you will speak only to the thoughtful reader. And more times than once you will ask yourself whether such readers really exist at all and why you should go on projecting your words into silence like an old crazy actor playing the part of himself to an empty theater.

The readers do exist. Jacques Barzun confidently guesses that there are at least thirty thousand of them in the United States, though they may have to be found vertically through many years rather than horizontally in any one publishing season, and though the hope of your reaching them all is about like the possibility of your tracking down all the surviving elk in America. But any of them you find you will treasure. This audience, by and large, will listen to what you say and not demand that you say what everyone else is saying or what some fashionable school or clique says you should say. They are there, scattered through the apparently empty theater, listening and making very little noise. Be grateful for them. But however grateful you are, never, never write to please them.

The moment you start consciously writing for an audience, you begin wondering if you are saying what the audience wants or expects. The peculiar virtue of this audience is that it leaves up to you what should be said. You have heard Frank O'Connor speak of the difference between the private and the public arts. Unless it is being dramatized or read aloud over the radio, fiction is one of the private ones. The audience has nothing to do with its making or with the slant it takes. You don't discover what should go into your novel by taking a poll or having a trial run in Boston or Philadelphia. You discover it by thinking and feeling your way into a situation or having it feel its way into you. From inside a web of relationships, from the very heart of a temperament, your imagination creates outward and forward.

You write to satisfy yourself and the inevitabilities of the situation you have started in motion. You write under a compulsion, it is true, but it is the compulsion of your situation, not of a private hatred or envy or fear; and you write to satisfy yourself, but you write always in the remote awareness of a listener— O'Connor's man in the armchair. He responds to what you respond to and understands what you understand. Above all, he listens. Being outside of you, he closes a circuit, he is an ear to your mouth. Unless at least one like him reads you, you have written uselessly. Your book is as hypothetical as the sound of the tree that falls in the earless forest.

Nevertheless, I repeat, except for vaguely imagining him and hoping he is there, ignore him, do not write what you think he would like. Write what *you* like. When your book is published, you will have a letter from at least one of him, perhaps from as many as twenty or thirty of him. With luck, as other books come on his numbers will grow. But to you he will always be a solitary reader, an ear, not an audience. Literature speaks to temperament, Conrad says. Your books will find the temperaments they can speak to.

And I would not blame you if you still asked, Why bother to make contact with kindred spirits you never see and may never hear from, who perhaps do not even exist except in your hopes? Why spend ten years in an apprenticeship to fiction only to discover that this society so little values what you do that it won't pay you a living wage for it?

Well, what goes on in your novel—the affectionate revelation of a relationship, the unraveling of the threads of love and interest binding a family together, the tranquil and not so tranquil emotions surrounding the death of a beloved and distinguished grandfather—this is closer to what happens in church than to what happens in the theater. Fiction always moves toward one or another of its poles, toward drama at one end or philosophy at the other. This book of yours is less entertainment than philosophical meditation presented in terms of personalities in action. It is serious, even sad; its colors and lights are autumnal. You have not loved Chekhov for nothing—maybe you imagined him as your reader in the armchair. He would listen while you told him the apparently simple thing you want to say: how love lasts, but changes, how life is full of heats and frustrations, causes and triumphs, and death is cool and quiet. It does not sound like much, summarized, and yet it embodies everything you believe about yourself and about human life and at least some aspects of the people you have most loved. In your novel, anguish and resignation are almost in balance. Your people live on the page and in the memory, because they have been loved and therefore have been richly imagined.

Your book is dramatized belief; and because in everyday life we make few contacts as intimate as this with another temperament and another mind, these scenes have an effect of cool shock—first almost embarrassment, then acknowledgment. Yes, I want to say. Yes, this is how it would be.

I like the sense of intimate knowing that your novel gives me. After all, what are any of us after but the conviction of belonging? What does more to stay us and keep our backbones stiff while the world reels than the sense that we are linked with someone who listens and understands and so in some way completes us? I have said somewhere else that the aesthetic experience is a conjugal act, like love. I profoundly believe it.

The worst thing that could happen to the ferocious seekers after identity is that they should find it and it only. There are many who do their best to escape it. Of our incorrigible and profound revulsion against identity, I suppose that physical love is the simplest, most immediate, and for many the only expression. Some have their comfort in feeling that they belong to the world of nature, big brother to the animals and cousin to the trees; some commit themselves to the kingdom of God. There is much in all of them, but for you, I imagine, not enough in any. For you it will have to be the kingdom of man, it will have to be art. You have nothing to gain and nothing to give except as you distill and purify ephemeral experience into quiet, searching, touching little stories like the one you have just finished, and so give your uncommon readers a chance to join you in the solidarity of pain and love and the vision of human possibility.

But isn't it enough? For lack of the full heart's desire, won't it serve?

(1982)

JOHN IRVING (b. 1942)

"GETTING STARTED"

Born John Wallace Blunt, Jr. in Exeter, New Hampshire in 1942, John Irving began his career as a writer at the age of twenty-six when his first novel, *Setting Free the Bears*, was published to a warm critical reception, but very little commercial success. It was not until 1978 that Irving published his great masterpiece, *The World According to Garp*, and thus secured his reputation as one of America's greatest contemporary writers. All of Irving's later novels have achieved bestseller status, including *The Cider House Rules* (1985), *A Prayer for Owen Meany* (1989), and *A Widow for One Year* (1998). In 1999, Irving won the Academy Award for Best Adapted Screenplay for *The Cider House Rules*. John Irving continues to live and write at his homes in Toronto, Ontario and southern Vermont.

As the title suggests, what follows is an essay on how to begin a novel. Extremely practical, it offers suggestions for opening lines and story planning, with many useful examples taken from literature and Irving's own work. And while sharing his own methods for opening a story, Irving slips in several other intriguing ideas on the art of writing.

It is useful when you begin a novel to evoke certain guidelines if not actual rules that have given you aid and comfort during the periods of tribulation that marked the beginnings of your Novels Past. You are never, of course, so given to imperatives as when you don't know what you're doing and, therefore, haven't begun. This helps to explain an obvious contradiction in most book reviews: a notable absence of any understanding of the examined work in tandem with a flood of imperatives regarding what the work ought to have been. First novelists, especially, are afflicted with the need to give advice—witness Tom Wolfe's advice to us all, regarding our proper subject matter (lest we end up bantering among ourselves, like so many poets). But I digress, a common weakness with all beginnings.

143

Beginnings are important. Here is a useful rule for beginning: Know the story—as much of the story as you can possibly know, if not the whole story—before you commit yourself to the first paragraph. Know the story—the whole story, if possible—before you fall in love with your first *sentence,* not to mention your first chapter. If you don't know the story before you begin the story, what kind of a storyteller are you? Just an ordinary kind, just a mediocre kind—making it up as you go along, like a common liar. Or else, to begin a novel without an ending fixed in your mind's eye, you must be very clever, and so full of confidence in the voice that tells the story that the story itself hardly matters. In my own case, I am much more plodding; confidence comes from knowing the story that lies ahead, not in the limited powers of the voice that tells it. This calls for patience, and for plotting.

And most of all, when beginning, be humble. Remember that your first, blank page has this in common with all other blank pages: it has not read your previous works. Don't be enthralled by the sound of your own voice; write with a purpose; have a plan. Know the story, *then* begin the story. Here endeth the lesson.

The authority in the storyteller's voice derives from fore-knowledge. In my opinion, a novel is written with predestina-tion—a novel being defined as a *narrative.* A *good* narrative has a *plot.* If you're not interested in plot, why write a novel? Because plot provides momentum, plot is what makes a novel better on page three hundred than it was on page thirty—*if* it's a good novel. A good novel, by definition, keeps getting better. Plot is what draws the reader in—plot *and* the development of characters who are worthy of the reader's emotional interest. Here endeth another lesson.

Is this advice for everyone? Of course not! "Plot" isn't what compels many novelists to write, or some readers to read. But if you choose to write a novel without a plot, I would hope three things for you: that your prose is gorgeous, that your insights into the human condition are inspirational, and that your book is short. I am directing my remarks, of course, to those writers (and readers) of *long* novels.

Would a film director begin to shoot a picture without a
screenplay? I would never begin a novel without knowing the
whole story; but even then, the choices for how to begin are
not simple. *You* may know exactly where the story begins, but
choosing where you want the *reader* to begin the story is another matter. And here cometh another lesson for the writer of
long novels: Think of the reader. Who is this reader? I think of
the reader as far more intelligent than I am, but a child—a
kind of hyperactive prodigy, a reading wizard. Interest this
child and he will put up with anything—he will understand
everything, too. But fail to seize and hold this child's attention,
at the beginning, and he will never come back to you. This is
your reader: paradoxically, a genius with the attention span of
a rabbit.

I am amazed that mere consideration of the reader, nowa-
days, often marks a writer as "commercial"—as opposed to "literary." To the snotty charge that Dickens wrote what the public
wanted, Chesterton replied, "Dickens *wanted* what the public
wanted!" Let us quickly clear up this name-calling regarding
"commercial" and "literary": it is for artistic reasons, in addition
to financial wisdom, that *any* author would prefer keeping a
reader's attention to losing it.

Three obvious but painstaking components either succeed in
making a novel "literary," or they fail and make it a mess: namely, the craftsmanlike quality of the storytelling (of course, in my
opinion, a novel should be a story worth telling); the true-to-life
quality of the characters (I also expect the characters to be skill-
fully developed); and the meticulous exactitude of the language
(discernible in every sentence and seeming to be spoken by an
unmistakable voice).

What makes a novel "commercial" is that a lot of people buy
it and finish it and tell other people to read it; both "literary"
novels and failed, messy novels can be commercially successful
or unsuccessful. The part about the reader *finishing* a novel is
important for the book's commercial success; both good reviews
and the author's preexistent popularity can put a book on the
best-seller lists, but what keeps a book on the list for a long time
is that a lot of those first readers actually finish the book and tell

their friends that they simply must read it. We don't tell our friends that they simply must read a book we're unable to finish.

In my own judgment, as a reader, the faults of most novels are the sentences—either they're ambitious or they're so unclear that they need to be rewritten. And what's wrong with the rest of the novels I don't finish is that the stories aren't good enough to merit writing a novel in the first place.

One of the pleasures of reading a novel is anticipation. Would a playwright *not* bother to anticipate what the audience is anticipating? The reader of a novel also enjoys the feeling that he can anticipate where the story is going; however, if the reader actually does anticipate the story, he is bored. The reader must be able to anticipate, but the reader must also guess wrong. How can an author make a reader anticipate—not to mention make a reader guess wrong—if the author himself doesn't *know* where the story is going? A good beginning will suggest knowledge of the whole story; it will give a strong hint regarding where the whole story is headed; yet a good beginning must be misleading, too.

Therefore, where to begin? Begin where the reader will be invited to do the most anticipating of the story, but where the reader will be the most compelled to guess wrong. If anticipation is a pleasure, so is surprise.

My last rule is informed by a remark of the late John Cheever—in his journals—that he was "forced to consider [his] prose by the ignobility of some of [his] material." My advice is to consider—from the beginning—that *all* of your material suffers from ignobility. Therefore, *always* consider your prose!

In the past, I have deliberately loaded my first sentences with all these admonitions in mind. The first sentence of *The World According to Garp:* "Garp's mother, Jenny Fields, was arrested in Boston in 1942 for wounding a man in a movie theater." (The sentence is a shameless tease; "wounded" is deliberately unclear—we want to know *how* the man was "wounded"—and that the person "arrested" was somebody's *mother* surely suggests a lurid tale.) The first sentence of *The Hotel New Hampshire:* "The summer my father bought the bear, none of us was born—we weren't even conceived: not Frank, the oldest;

not Franny, the loudest; not me, the next; and not the youngest of us, Lilly and Egg." (Well, what is shameless about this is that *anybody* bought a bear. The rest of the sentence is simply an economical means of introducing the members of a large family. In fact, this family is so large, it is cumbersome; therefore, a few of them will die deaths of convenience rather early in the novel.) The first sentence of *The Cider House Rules:* "In the hospital of the orphanage—the boy's division at St. Cloud's, Maine—two nurses were in charge of naming the new babies and checking that their little penises were healing from the obligatory circumcision." (This beginning operates on the assumption that orphanages are emotionally engaging to everyone; also, how people are named is always interesting, and the matter of "obligatory circumcision" suggests either religion or eccentricity—or both. Besides, I always wanted to put "penises" in an opening sentence; the word, I suppose, sends a signal that this novel is *not* for everyone.) And the first sentence of *A Prayer for Owen Meany:* "I am doomed to remember a boy with a wrecked voice—not because of his voice, or because he was the smallest person I ever knew, or even because he was the instrument of my mother's death, but because he is the reason I believe in God; I am a Christian because of Owen Meany." (When in doubt, or wherever possible, tell the whole story of the novel in the first sentence.)

All of those first sentences were not simply the first sentences I ended up with; they were, with one exception, the first sentence of those books that I wrote. (In the case of *Garp*, the *first* first sentence was the sentence that is now the last sentence of the book: "But in the world according to Garp, we are all terminal cases.")

In the case of the novel I am now writing, I have narrowed the possible beginning to three choices; I haven't made up my mind among these choices—so it is still possible that a fourth alternative will present itself, and be chosen, but I doubt it. I think I shall proceed with something very close to one of these.

1. "A widow for one year, Ruth Cole was forty-six; a novelist for twenty years (counting from 1970, when her first book was

published), she'd been famous only a little longer than she'd been a widow—in fact, in Mrs. Cole's mind, her husband's death and her literary success were so closely associated that her grief overshadowed any enjoyment she could take from the world's newfound appreciation of her work."

This is a plain, old-fashioned beginning: it holds back more than it tells, and I like that. The character is a woman of some achievement; we may therefore expect her to be a character of some complexity, and—as a recent widow—we can be assured that we enter her life at a vulnerable moment. This beginning continues to build on our impression of Mrs. Cole *at this moment*.

"Furthermore, she'd always perceived any recognition of her writing—both when the praise had been spotty and now that it was profuse—as nothing more than a seductive invasion of her privacy; that such sudden and so much attention should come to her at a time when she most sought to be alone (and most needed to grow accustomed to being alone) was simply annoying. Fame, to Mrs. Cole, was merely a trivial vexation among the more painful torments of her loneliness. She wanted her husband alive again, she wanted him back; for it was only in her life with him that she'd been afforded the greatest privacy, not to mention an intimacy she'd never taken for granted."

We stand on solid ground with this beginning; we already know a lot about Mrs. Cole and her situation. We may be interested in such a woman, at such a time in her life, but there is no hook; the beginning is *too* plain—it lacks even a hint of anything sensational.

Try again.

2. "Dr. Daruwalla had upsetting news for the famous actor, Inspector Dutt; not sure of the degree to which Inspector Dutt would be distressed, Dr. Daruwalla was impelled by cowardice to give the movie star the bad news in a public place—young Dutt's extraordinary poise in public was renowned; the doctor felt he could rely on the actor to keep his composure."

This, of course, is the beginning of a novel by Ruth Cole; it is one of *her* beginnings. Mrs. Cole continues in a tone of voice that promises us she will, occasionally, be funny. "Not everyone in Bombay would have thought of a private club as a 'public place,' but Dr. Daruwalla believed that the choice was both private and public enough for the particular crisis at hand." And the second paragraph provides the "hook" I feel is missing from my first beginning.

"That morning when Dr. Daruwalla arrived at the Duckworth Sports and Eating Club, he thought it was unremarkable to see a vulture high in the sky above the golf course; he did not consider the bird of death as an omen attached to the unwelcome burden of the news he carried. The club was in Mahalaxmi, not far from Malabar Hill; everyone in Bombay knew why the vultures were attracted to Malabar Hill. When a corpse was placed in the Towers of Silence, the vultures—from thirty miles outside Bombay—could scent the ripening remains."

This is certainly a more mysterious beginning than my first—not to mention more foreign. The language (that is, Mrs. Cole's) is more lush and dense than my own—this beginning is altogether more exotic. But pity the poor reader when he discovers that this is *not* the novel he is reading; rather, it is a novel *within* the novel he is reading. Won't the poor reader feel misled too much? (To mislead is divine, to *trick* is another matter!) However, I am aware that I will never get the reader to read Mrs. Cole's Indian novel as closely as I want him to *if* the reader knows it is merely a novel within a novel; by beginning with Mrs. Cole's novel, I make the reader read it closely. What a choice! And so I come, cautiously in the middle, to the third possibility.

3. "*Son of the Circus,* the seventh novel by the American novelist Ruth Cole, was first published in the United States in September 1989; the excitement was mitigated for the author by the unexpected death of her husband—he died in his sleep beside his wife, in a hotel in New York City; they had just begun the promotion tour."

This is not yet quite the blend I want—between what is plain and old-fashioned, and what is exotic—but it comes close to satisfying me, *provided that* I begin the so-called Indian novel quickly, before the reader becomes *too* involved in poor Mrs.

Cole's widowhood (not to mention the bad timing of her husband's demise). And that last line—"they had just begun the promotion tour"—hints at a tone of voice that will prevail both in Ruth Cole's fiction and in my telling of her actual story; any consideration of one's prose must include a consideration of the tone of voice.

But what I miss (from Mrs. Cole's beginning) is greater than the kind of purity gained by the third possibility. Both the first and third beginnings tell the reader what *has* happened to Ruth Cole; Mrs. Cole, on the other hand, tells us what Dr. Daruwalla is *going to* do—he's going to give an actor named Inspector Dutt some bad news. What *is* this news? I want to know. And Dr. Daruwalla may be so used to vultures that *he* does "not consider the bird of death as an omen," but we readers know better: of *course* the vulture is an omen! *Anyone* knows that! Therefore, at this writing, I am inclined to begin my novel with Mrs. Cole's first chapter, or part of it. If Mrs. Cole's story is good enough, the reader will forgive me for my trick.

Even as I write, a fourth opportunity presents itself to me: instead of starting with Mrs. Cole's novel or with Mrs. Cole, it is possible to begin with someone else reading her novel—perhaps her former lover.

"At that moment, the German stopped reading; he was a golfer himself, he did not find dead-golfer jokes amusing, and he was overwhelmed by the density of the description—the pace of this novel was unbearably slow for him, not to mention how little interested he was in India. He was not much of a reader, especially not of novels, and he despaired that he was less than halfway through the first chapter of a very long novel and already he was bored. (The last book he'd read was about golf.) But special interests, none of them literary, would compel him to keep reading the novel he'd momentarily put aside.

"He knew the author; that is, he had briefly been her lover, many years ago, and he was vain enough to imagine that in her novel he would find some trace of himself—that was what he was reading for. Once he penetrated the story—past the dead golfer—he would find much more than he'd bargained for; his imagination simply wasn't up to the task he'd set for himself, but he didn't know that as he sat fingering the German translation and smiling boorishly at the author photograph, which he found faintly arousing."

And by the time you read this, I may be considering a fifth possibility. Anyway, once the beginning is locked in place, it is time to invite similar scrutiny of the next chapter and then the next. With any luck, you will hear from me (and Mrs. Cole) in about four years.

(1991)

Joyce Carol Oates (b. 1938)

"Running and Writing"

Joyce Carol Oates was born on June 16, 1938 in Lockport, New York. A gifted writer since youth, Oates wrote for her high school newspaper, won a scholarship to study at Syracuse University, and won *Mademoiselle* magazine's "college short story" contest when she was nineteen years old. She began her prolific career as a professional writer with the 1964 publication of her first novel, *With Shuddering Fall*. In 1970, Oates received the National Book Award for her fourth novel, *them*, before going on to produce over thirty novels, twenty-nine short story collections, numerous plays, non-fiction writings, poetry collections, and children's books. Joyce Carol Oates continues to write, and is currently the Roger S. Berlind Distinguished Professor of the Humanities at Princeton University.

Perhaps the quirkiest essay in this collection, "Running and Writing" is about just that: running and writing. Tracing her history as an avid jogger, Oates describes how motion (of all speeds) parallels, informs, and inspires her fiction. Even for the writer who is not so keen on excercise, this piece offers fascinating advice on how to overcome writer's block and motivate oneself not only to write, but to write well.

Running! If there's any activity happier, more exhilarating, more nourishing to the imagination, I can't think what it might be. In running, the mind flies with the body; the mysterious efflorescence of language seems to pulse in the brain, in rhythm with our feet and the swinging of our arms. Ideally, the runner-who's-a-writer is running through the land- and cityscapes of her fiction, like a ghost in a real setting.

There must be some analogue between running and dreaming. The dreaming mind is usually bodiless, has peculiar powers of locomotion and, in my experience at least, often runs or glides or "flies" along the ground, or in the air. (Leaving aside the blunt, deflating theory that dreams are merely compensatory: you fly in sleep because in life you crawl, barely; you're soaring above others in sleep because in life others soar above you.) Possibly these fairy-tale feats of locomotion are atavistic remnants, the hallucinatory memory of a distant ancestor for whom the physical being, charged with adrenaline in emergency situations, was indistinguishable from the spiritual or intellectual. In running, "spirit" seems to pervade the body; as musicians experience the uncanny phenomenon of tissue memory in their fingertips, so the runner seems to experience in feet, lungs, quickened heartbeat, an extension of the imagining self. The structural problems I set for myself in writing, in a long, snarled, frustrating and sometimes despairing morning of work, for instance, I can usually unsnarl by running in the afternoon. On days when I can't run, I don't feel "myself" and whoever the "self" is I do feel, I don't like nearly so much as the other. And the writing remains snarled in endless revisions.

Writers and poets are famous for loving to be in motion. If not running, hiking; if not hiking, walking. (Walking, even fast, is a poor second to running, as all runners know, that we'll resort to when our knees go, but at least it's an option.) The great English Romantic poets were clearly inspired by their long walks, in all weather: Wordsworth and Coleridge in the idyllic Lake District, for instance; Shelley ("I always go until I am stopped and I never am stopped") in his four intense years in Italy. The New England Transcendentalists, most famously Henry David Thoreau, were ceaseless walkers; Thoreau boasted of having "traveled much in Concord," and in his eloquent essay "Walking" acknowledged that he had to spend more than four hours out-of-doors daily, in motion; otherwise he felt "as if I had some sin to be atoned for." My favorite prose on the subject is Charles Dickens's "Night Walks," which Dickens wrote some years after having suffered extreme insomnia that propelled him out into the London streets at night. Written with Dickens's usual brilliance, this haunting essay seems to hint at more than its words reveal; Dickens associates his terrible night-restlessness with being unhoused, thus out of character; his new, impersonal identity he calls "Houselessness"—under a compulsion to walk, and walk, and walk in the darkness and pattering rain. (No one has captured the romance of desolation, the ecstasy of near-madness, more forcibly than Dickens, so wrongly interpreted as a dispenser of popular, soft-hearted tales.) It isn't surprising that Walt Whitman should have tramped impressive distances, for you can feel the pulse-beat of the walker in his slightly breathless, incantatory poems, but it may be surprising to learn that Henry James, who for all his prose style more resembles the fussy intricacies of crocheting than the fluidity of movement, also loved to walk for miles in London.

I, too, walked (and ran) for miles in London, years ago. Much of it in Hyde Park. Regardless of weather! Living for a sabbatical year with my English professor husband in a corner of Mayfair overlooking Speakers' Corner, I was so afflicted with homesickness for America, and for Detroit, I ran compulsively; not as a respite for the intensity of writing, but as a function of writing, for as I ran I was running in Detroit, envisioning the city's parks and streets, avenues and expressways, with such eidetic clarity, I had only to transcribe them when I returned to our flat, re-creating Detroit in my novel *Do With Me What You Will* as faithfully as I'd re-created Detroit in *them,* when I was living there. What a curious experience! Without the bouts of running, I don't believe I could have written the novel; yet how perverse, one thinks, to be living in one of the world's most beautiful cities, London, and to be dreaming of one of the world's most problematic cities, Detroit.

Both running and writing are highly addictive activities; both are, for me, inextricably bound up with consciousness. I can't recall a time when I wasn't running, and I can't recall a time when I wasn't writing. (Before I could write what might be called human words in the English language, I eagerly emulated grown-ups' handwriting in pencil scribbles. My first "novels"— which, I'm afraid, my loving parents still have, in a trunk or a drawer on our old farm property in Millersport, New York— were tablets of inspired scribbles illustrated by line drawings of chickens, horses, and upright cats. For I had not yet mastered the trickier human form, as I was years from mastering human psychology.) My earliest outdoor memories have to do with the special solitude of running or hiking in our pear and apple orchards, through fields of wind-rustling corn towering over my head, along farmers' lanes and on bluffs above the Tonawanda Creek. Through childhood I hiked, roamed, tirelessly "explored" the countryside; neighboring farms, a treasure trove of old barns, abandoned houses and forbidden properties of all kinds, some of them presumably dangerous, like cisterns and wells covered with loose boards. These activities are intimately bound up with storytelling, for always there's a ghost-self, a "fictitious" self, in such settings. For this reason I believe that any form of art is a species of exploration and transgression. (I never saw a NO TRESPASSING sign that wasn't a summons to my rebellious blood. Such signs, dutifully posted on trees and fence railings, might as well cry COME RIGHT IN!) To write is to invade another's space, if only to memorialize it; to write is to invite angry censure from those who don't write, or who don't write in quite the way you do, for whom you may seem a threat. Art by its nature is a transgressive act, and artists must accept being punished for it. The more original and unsettling their art, the more devastating the punishment.

If writing involves punishment, at least for some of us, the act of running even in adulthood can evoke painful memories of having been, long ago, as children, chased by tormentors. (Is there any adult who hasn't such memories? Are there any adult women who have not been, in one way or another, sexually molested or threatened?) That adrenaline rush like an injection to the heart! I attended a one-room country schoolhouse in which eight very disparate grades were taught by a single overworked woman teacher; the teasing, pummeling, pinching, punching, mauling and kicking and verbal abuse that surrounded the relative sanctuary of the schoolhouse simply had to be endured, for in those days there were no protective laws against such mistreatment; this was a laissez-faire era in which a man might beat his wife and children, and police would rarely intervene except in cases of serious injuries or deaths. Often when I'm running in the most idyllic landscapes, I'm reminded of the panicked childhood running of decades ago; I was one of those luckless children without older brothers or sisters to protect her against the systematic cruelty of older classmates, thus fair game. I don't believe I was singled out (because my grades were high, for instance) and came to see years later that such abuse is generic, not personal; it must prevail through the species; it allows us insight into the experiences of others, a sense of what a more enduring panic, entrapment, suffering, and despair must be truly like. Sexual abuse seems to us the most repellent kind of abuse, and it's certainly the abuse that nourishes a palliative amnesia.

Beyond the lines of printed words in my books are the settings in which the books were imagined and without which the books could not exist. Sometime in 1985, for instance, running along the Delaware River south of Yardley, Pennsylvania, I glanced up and saw the ruins of a railroad bridge, and experienced in a flash such a vivid, visceral memory of crossing a footbridge beside a similar railroad trestle high above the Erie Canal, in Lockport, New York, when I was twelve to fourteen years old, that I saw the possibility of a novel; this would become *You Must Remember This,* set in a mythical upstate New York city very like the original. Yet often the reverse occurs: I find myself running in a place so intriguing to me, amid houses, or the backs of houses, so mysterious, I'm fated to write about these sights, to bring them to life (as it's said) in fiction. I'm a writer absolutely mesmerized by places; much of my writing is a way of assuaging homesickness, and the settings my characters inhabit are as crucial to me as the characters themselves. I couldn't write even a very short story without vividly "seeing" what its characters see.

Stories come to us as wraiths requiring precise embodiments. Running seems to allow me, ideally, an expanded consciousness in which I can envision what I'm writing as a film or a dream; I rarely invent at the typewriter, but recall what I've experienced; I don't use a word processor, but write in longhand, at considerable length. (Again, I know: Writers are crazy.) By the time I come to type out my writing formally I've envisioned it repeatedly. I've never thought of writing as the mere arrangement of words on the page but the attempted embodiment of a vision; a complex of emotions; raw experience. The effort of memorable art is to evoke in the reader or spectactor emotions appropriate to that effort. Running is a meditation; more practicably, it allows me to scroll through, in my mind's eye, the pages I've just written, proofreading for errors and improvements. My method is one of continuous revision; while writing a long novel, every day I loop back to earlier sections, to rewrite, in order to maintain a consistent, fluid voice; when I write the final two or three chapters of a novel, I write them simultaneously with the rewriting of the opening of the novel, so that, ideally at least, the novel is like a river uniformly flowing, each passage concurrent with all the others. Dreams may be temporary flights into madness that, by some law of neurophysiology unclear to us, keep us from actual madness; so too the twin activities of running/writing keep the writer reasonably sane, and with the hope, however illusory and temporary, of control.

(1999)

MARGARET ATWOOD (b. 1939)

"NOBODY TO NOBODY"

Margaret Atwood was born in Ontario, Canada in 1939, where she spent most of her childhood between Ottawa, Toronto, and the forests of northern Ontario. Although she began writing plays and poems at the age of six, Atwood did not begin to write seriously until the age of sixteen, and in 1957 began her studies at the University of Toronto. Her first publication was the privately printed book of poems, *Double Persephone*, for which she won the E. J. Pratt Medal. Considered one of Canada's greatest living writers, her novels include *The Handmaid's Tale* (1985), *Cat's Eye* (1988), *Oryx and Crake* (2003), and her most recent novel, *The Penelopiad* (2005). She currently lives and writes in Toronto and Peelee Island, Ontario.

The following essay is an analysis of, and reflection on, the communication between the writer, the reader, and the work of fiction. In this triangle, the writer and reader cannot communicate directly, but rather each must look to the text as the message that passes among them. Exploring this relationship, Atwood elucidates how the writer must craft his text carefully, always keeping the reader in mind, so that the message becomes precisely the story that was originally envisioned.

> How pleased therefore will the reader be to find that we have, in the following work, adhered closely to one of the highest principles of the best cook which the present age, or perhaps that of Heliogabulus, hath produced . . . By this means, we doubt not but our reader may be rendered desirous to read on for ever, as the great person, just above-mentioned, is supposed to have made some persons eat.
>
> Henry Fielding, *Tom Jones*[1]

A man listening to a story is in the company of the storyteller; even a man reading one shares this companionship. The reader of a novel, however, is isolated, more so than any other reader . . .

In this solitude of his, the reader of a novel seizes upon his material more jealously than anyone else. He is ready to make it his own, to devour it, as it were.
        Walter Benjamin, "The Storyteller"[2]

As Detlov von Liliencron wrote, his rhymes dripping with sarcasm: it is hard for the poet to evade fame. If he cannot secure the favor of the masses in his lifetime, posterity will praise his heroic way of starving to death. In a word, to sell was to sell out.
        Peter Gay, *The Pleasure Wars*[3]

. . . for we are great statements in our days
and on the basis of that we can expect small audiences.
        Gwendolyn MacEwen, "The Choice"[4]

The big blundering newspaper had discovered him, and now he was proclaimed and anointed and crowned. His place was assigned to him as publicly as if a fat usher with a wand had pointed to the topmost chair . . . In a flash, somehow, all was different; the tremendous wave I speak of had swept something away. It had knocked down, I suppose, my little customary altar, my twinkling tapers and my flowers, and had reared itself into a temple vast and bare. When Neil Paraday should come out of the house he would come out a contemporary. That was what had happened: the poor man was to be squeezed into his horrible age.
        Henry James, "The Death of the Lion"[5]

I rip the envelope and I'm in Bangkok
. . . You pour from these squares, these blue envoys.
And just when I feel I've lost you to the world,
I can't keep up,
Your postcard comes with the words
"wait for me."
        Anne Michaels, "Letters from Martha"[6]

I would like to begin by talking about messengers. Messengers always exist in a triangular situation—the one who sends the message, the message-bearer, whether human or inorganic, and the one who receives the message. Picture, therefore, a triangle, but not a complete triangle: something more like an upside-down V. The writer and the reader are at the two lateral corners, but there's no line joining them. Between them—whether above or below—is a third point, which is the written word, or the text, or the book, or the poem, or the letter, or whatever you would like to call it. This third point is the only point of contact between the other two. As I used to say to my writing students in the distant days when I had some, "Respect the page. It's all you've got."

The writer communicates with the page. The reader also communicates with the page. The writer and the reader communicate only through the page. This is one of the syllogisms of writing as such. Pay no attention to the facsimiles of the writer that appear on talkshows, in newspaper interviews, and the like—they ought not to have anything to do with what goes on between you, the reader, and the page you are reading, where an invisible hand has previously left some marks for you to decipher, much as one of John Le Carré's dead spies has left a waterlogged shoe with a small packet in it for George Smiley.[7] I know this is a far-fetched image, but it is also curiously apt, since the reader is—among other things—a sort of spy. A spy, a trespasser, someone in the habit of reading other people's letters and diaries. As Northrop Frye has implied, the reader does not hear, he overhears.[8]

So far I've spoken primarily about writers. Now it's the turn of readers, more or less. The questions I would like to pose are, first: for whom does the writer write? And, secondly: what is the book's function—or duty, if you like—in its position between writer and reader? What ought it to be doing, in the opinion of its writer? And finally, a third question arising from the other two: where is the writer when the reader is reading?

If you really are in the habit of reading other people's letters and diaries, you'll know the answer to that one straightaway: when you are reading, the writer is *not in the same room.* If he were, either you'd be talking together, or he'd catch you in the act.

For whom does the writer write? The question poses itself most simply in the case of the diary-writer or journal-keeper. Only very occasionally is the answer specifically *no one,* but this is a misdirection, because we couldn't hear it unless a writer had put it in a book and published it for us to read. Here for instance is diary-writer Doctor Glas, from Hjalmar Söderberg's astonishing 1905 Swedish novel of the same name:

> Now I sit at my open window, writing—for whom? Not for any friend or mistress. Scarcely for myself, even. I do not read today what I wrote yesterday; nor shall I read this tomorrow. I write simply so my hand can move, my thoughts move of their own accord. I write to kill a sleepless hour.[9]

A likely story, and it *is* a likely story—we, the readers, believe it easily enough. But the truth—the real truth, the truth behind the illusion—is that the writing is not by Doctor Glas, and it's not addressed to no one. It's by Hjalmar Söderberg, and it's addressed to us.

The fictional writer who writes to no one is rare. More usually, even fictional writers writing fictional journals wish to suppose a reader. Here is a passage from George Orwell's *Nineteen Eighty-Four,* a book I read as a young person, shortly after it first came out in 1949. As we know, *Nineteen Eighty-Four* takes place in a grimy totalitarian future ruled by Big Brother. The hero, Winston Smith, has seen in a junk-store window a forbidden object: "a thick, quarto-sized blank book with a red back and a marbled cover" and "smooth creamy paper."[10] He has been seized by the desire to possess this book, despite the dangers that owning it would entail. Who among writers has not been overcome by a similar desire? And who has not been aware, too, of the dangers—specifically, the dangers of self-revelation? Because if you get hold of a blank book, especially one with creamy pages, you will be driven to write in it. And this is what Winston Smith does, with a real pen and real ink, because the lovely paper deserves these. But then a question arises:

> For whom, it suddenly occurred to him to wonder, was he writing this diary? For the future, for the unborn . . . for the first time the magnitude of what he had undertaken came home to him. How could you communicate with the future? It was of its nature impossible. Either the future would resemble the present, in which case it would not listen to him: or it would be different from it, and his predicament would be meaningless.[11]

A common writerly dilemma: who's going to read what you

write, now or ever? Who do you want to read it? Winston Smith's first readership is himself—it gives him satisfaction to write his forbidden thoughts in his diary. When I was a teenager, this account of Winston Smith's blank book was intensely attractive to me. I too attempted to keep such a diary, without result. My failure was my failure to imagine a reader. I didn't want anybody else to read my diary—only I should have access to it. But I myself already knew the sorts of things I might put into it, and mawkish things they were, so why bother writing them down? It seemed a waste of time. But many have not found it so. Countless are the diaries and journals, most obscure, some famous, that have been faithfully kept through the centuries, or the centuries of pen and paper, at least. For whom was Samuel Pepys writing? Or Saint-Simon? Or Anne Frank? There is something magical about such real-life documents. The fact that they have survived, have reached our hands, seems like the delivery of an unexpected treasure; or else like a resurrection.

These days I do manage to keep a journal of sorts, more in self-defense than anything else, because I know who the reader will be: it will be myself, in about three weeks, because I can no longer remember what I might have been doing at any given time. The older one gets, the more relevant Beckett's play *Krapp's Last Tape* comes to be. In this play, Krapp is keeping a journal on tape, from year to year. His only reader—or auditor—is himself, as he plays back bits of the tapes from his earlier lives. As time goes on, he has a harder and harder time identifying the person he is now with his former selves. It's like that bad stockbrokers' joke about Alzheimer's Disease—at least you keep meeting new people—but in Krapp's case, and increasingly in mine, you yourself are those new people.

The private diary is about as minimalist as you can get, in the writer-to-reader department, because writer and reader are assumed to be the same. It is also about as intimate, as a form. Next comes, I suppose, the private letter: one writer, one reader, and a shared intimacy. "This is my letter to the World / That never wrote to me," said Emily Dickinson.[12] Of course she might have got more replies if she'd mailed it. But she did intend a reader, or more than one, at least in the future: she saved her poems up very carefully, and even sewed them into little booklets. Her faith in the existence, indeed the attentiveness, of the future reader was the opposite of Winston Smith's despair.

Writers have of course made copious use of the letter as a form, inserting letters into the narrative, and in some cases building whole novels out of them, as Richardson did in *Pamela, Clarissa Harlowe,* and *Sir Charles Grandison,* and as Laclos did in *Les Liaisons dangereuses.* For the reader, the fictional exchange of letters among several individuals provides the delight of the secret agent listening in on a wire: letters have an immediacy that the past tense cannot provide, and the lies and manipulations of the characters can be caught in *flagrante delicto.* Or this is the idea.

A few words about letter-writing and the anxieties specific to it. When I was a child, there was a game that was popular at little girls' birthday parties. It went like this:

The children stood in a circle. One of them was It, and walked around the outside of the circle holding a handkerchief, while the others sang:

> I wrote a letter to my love
> And on the way I dropped it,
> A little doggie picked it up
> And put it in his pocket.

Then there was talk of dog-bites, and a moment when the handkerchief was dropped behind someone, followed by a chase around the outside of the circle. None of this part interested me. I was still worrying about the letter. How terrible that it had been lost, and that the person to whom it was written would never get it! How equally terrible that someone else had found it! My only consolation was that dogs can't read.

Ever since writing was invented, such accidents have been a distinct possibility. Once the words have been set down they form part of a material object, and as such must take their chances. The letter from the king that is exchanged, unknown to the messenger, causing an innocent person to be condemned to death—this is not merely an old folktale motif. Forged letters, letters gone astray and never received, letters that are destroyed, or that fall into the wrong hands—not only that, forged manuscripts, entire books that are lost and never read, books that are burned, books that fall into the hands of those who don't read them in the spirit in which they are written, or who do, but still resent them deeply—all these confusions and mistakes and acts of misapprehension and malice have taken place many times over, and continue to take place. In the lists of those targeted and imprisoned and killed by any dictatorship, there are always quite a few writers, whose works have reached—self-evidently—the wrong readers. A bullet in the neck is a very bad review.

But for every letter and every book, there is an intended reader, a true reader. How then to deliver the letter or book into the right hands? Winston Smith, writing his diary, finds he cannot be content with himself as his only reader. He chooses an ideal reader—a party official called O'Brien, in whom he believes he detects the signs of a subversiveness equal to his own. O'Brien, he feels, will understand him. He's right about this: his intended reader does understand him. O'Brien has already thought the thoughts that Winston Smith is thinking, but he's thought them in order to be prepared with the counter-moves, because O'Brien is a member of the secret police, and what he understands is that Winston is a traitor to the regime. He proceeds to arrest poor Winston, and then to destroy both his diary and his mind.

O'Brien is a negative or demonic version of Writer-to-Dear Reader, that ideal one-to-one relationship in which the person reading is exactly the person who ought to be reading. A more recent variation of the Demon Reader has been created by Stephen King, who specializes in extreme paranoia—and since he has a different kind of paranoia for every taste, he has a special one just for writers. The book is *Misery*,[13] and in it a writer of suffering-heroine romances featuring a hapless maiden called Misery falls into the hands of a deranged nurse who styles herself "your biggest fan." Veterans of book-signings would know right then to run for the washroom and escape out the window, but our hero can't do that, because he's been incapacitated in a car crash. What his "biggest fan" wants is to force him to write a book about Misery, just for her. Then, he realizes, she plans to bump him off so that this book will only ever have one reader—herself. It's a version of the sultan's-maze motif—used, among other places, in *The Phantom of the Opera*[14]—in which the patron of a work of art wishes to murder its maker so only he will possess its secrets. The hero of *Misery* escapes with his life after the required amount of guck has messed up the furniture, leaving us to reflect that the one-to-one Writer-to-Dear-Reader relationship can get altogether too close for comfort.

It is altogether too close for comfort as well when the reader confuses the writer with the text: such a reader wants to abolish the middle term, and to get hold of the text by getting hold of the writer, in the flesh. We assume too easily that a text exists to act as a communication between the writer and the reader. But doesn't it also act as a disguise, even a shield—a protection? The play *Cyrano de Bergerac*[15] features a large-nosed poet who expresses his love for the heroine by pretending to be someone else—but it is he who writes the eloquent letters that win her heart. Thus the book, as a form, expresses its own emotions and thoughts, while concealing from view the person who has concocted them. The difference between Cyrano and the book in general is that Cyrano gives vent to his own emotions, but the thoughts and emotions in a book are not necessarily those of the writer of it.

Despite the hazards a reader may pose, a reader must be postulated by a writer, and always is. Postulated, but rarely visualized in any exact, specific form—apart that is from the primary readers, who may be those named on the dedication page—"Mr. W. H.,"[16] or "my wife," and so forth—or the group of friends and editors thanked in the acknowledgments. But beyond that, the reader is the great unknown. Here is Emily Dickinson on the subject:

> I'm Nobody! Who are you?
> Are you—Nobody—Too?
> Then there's a pair of us!
> Don't tell!—they'd advertise—you know!

How dreary—to be—Somebody!
How public—like a Frog—
To tell one's name—the livelong June—
To an admiring Bog![17]

"Nobody" is the writer, and the reader is also Nobody. In that sense, all books are anonymous, and so are all readers. Reading and writing—unlike, for instance, acting and theatre-going—are both activities that presuppose a certain amount of solitude, even a certain amount of secrecy. I expect Emily Dickinson is using "Nobody" in both of its senses—in the sense of an insignificant person, a nobody, but also in the sense of the invisible and never-to-be-known writer, addressing the invisible and never-to-be-known reader.

If the writer is Nobody addressing the reader, who is another Nobody—that hypocrite reader who is his likeness and his brother, as Baudelaire remarked[18]—where do the dreary Somebody and the admiring Bog come into it?

Publication changes everything. "They'd advertise," warns Emily Dickinson, and how right she was. Once the catalog is out of the bag, the assumed readership cannot consist of just one person—a friend or a lover, or even a single unknown Nobody. With publication, the text replicates itself, and the reader is no longer an intimate, a one to your one. Instead the reader too multiplies, just like the copies of the book, and all those nobodies add up to the reading public. If the writer has a success, he becomes a Somebody, and the mass of readers becomes his admiring Bog. But turning from a nobody into a somebody is not without its traumas. The nobody-writer must throw off the cloak of invisibility and put on the cloak of visibility. As Marilyn Monroe is rumored to have said, "If you're nobody you can't be somebody unless you're somebody else."[19]

And then doubt sets in. The writer-while-writing and the Dear Reader assumed as the eventual recipient of this writing have a relationship that is quite different from that between the mass-produced edition and "the reading public." Dear Reader is singular—second-person singular. Dear Reader is a You. But once both book and Dear Reader become multiplied by thousands, the book becomes a publishing statistic, and Nobody can be quantified, and thus becomes a market, and turns into the great plural third-person Them, and Them is another thing altogether.

Becoming known to Them results in the condition known as Fame, and the attitudes to fame, and to being famous, changed radically from the end of the eighteenth century to the end of the nineteenth. In the eighteenth century, the readership was assumed to be educated, to have taste; Voltaire, for instance, saw his fame as a tribute to his talents, not as a minus factor. Even the early Romantics had nothing against fame; in fact, they longed for it. "The Trumpet of Fame is as a tower of Strength the ambitious bloweth it and is safe,"[20] said John Keats in a letter. But by the end of the century, a bigger slice of the public was literate, the dreaded bourgeoisie—not to mention the even more dreaded masses—now determined how many copies would sell, publishing had become a business, "fame" and "popularity" were equated, and to have a small but discriminating readership now had a definite appeal.

This attitude persisted well into the twentieth century. Here is a Graham Greene character from *The End of the Affair*—a rather grubby novelist called Maurice Bendrix, who knows he is about to commit the art-for-art-influenced blunder of becoming a "vulgar success."[21] This is what he thinks as he prepares to be interviewed by a critic who wants to write him up for a literary journal:

I knew too well . . . the buried significance he would discover of which I was unaware and the faults I was tired of facing. Patronizingly in the end he would place me—probably a little above Maugham because Maugham is popular and I have not yet committed that crime—not yet, but although I retain a little of the exclusiveness of unsuccess, the little reviews, like wise detectives, can scent it on its way.[22]

Greene is being satirical, but the attitude he is satirizing was real enough: popularity—too much of it—was still regarded as a crime if you aspired to being what used to be called a "highbrow" writer. In Cyril Connolly's *Enemies of Promise*, too much failure and too much success are equally to be feared. Among the other things a young writer has to look out for are his own potential readers, because once you start comforting yourself with the idea that they at least love you no matter what the critics say, you're finished as a serious writer. "Of all the enemies of literature, success is the most insidious,"[23] says Connolly. He then quotes Trollope: "'Success is a poison that should only be taken late in life, then only in small doses.'"[24] It seems churlish to remark that only successful people ever say things like that; but Connolly expounds. He breaks success down into social success: not too bad, because it can provide material; professional success: the regard of one's fellow artists, on the whole a good thing; and popular success, a grave danger. This last he also divides into three: a writer may become popular for his entertainment value, for political reasons, or because he has the human touch. Of these, the political factor is the least fatal to art, he thinks, because politics are volatile and complacency is therefore unlikely. An entertainer does not benefit from informed criticism because nobody ever offers any; his fate is simply to "go on and on until he wakes up one day to find himself obscure."[25] But those with the human touch may be ruined as artists: Connolly says, "Neither harsh reviews, the contempt of equals, nor the indifference of superiors can affect those who have once tapped the great heart of suffering humanity and found out what a goldmine it is."[26]

Connolly was not alone in his analysis; in fact, by his time— and by mine—this attitude was endemic among those with ambitions as artists. Take, for instance, Isak Dinesen's story, "The Young Man With the Carnation." It begins with a writer called Charlie who has achieved a remarkable success with his first novel, which was about the struggles of the poor. Now he feels like a fraud, because he doesn't know what to write next; he's sick of the poor, he doesn't want to hear another word about them, but his admirers and the public have decided he's noble, and are expecting yet more and better things about the poor from his pen. If he writes about anything else, they will think he's superficial and hollow. No matter what he does, he feels, he will be doomed—doomed to disappoint—to disappoint the public, the great Them. He wouldn't even be able to commit suicide with impunity: "Now he had had the glaring searchlight of renown set on him, a hundred eyes were watching him, and his failure or suicide would be the failure and the suicide of a world-famous author."[27]

There is no writer who has achieved any success at all who has not confronted this package of doubts. Repeat yourself and satisfy Them, or do something different and disappoint Them. Or worse—repeat yourself and satisfy Them, and then be accused of repetition.

There are certain stories you read—usually quite early in life—that take on an emblematic quality for you. One of these for me is a Ray Bradbury story from *The Martian Chronicles*, the title of which is "The Martian." It goes as follows:

The Americans have colonized Mars, and part of it has been turned into a sort of retirement town. The original Martians are possibly extinct, or have taken to the hills. A middle-aged American couple, who have lost their young son Tom back on Earth, hear a knock on their door in the middle of the night. A small boy is standing in the yard. He looks like the dead son. The man sneaks down and unlocks the door, and in the morning there is Tom, all fresh and shining. The man guesses it must be a Martian, but the wife accepts Tom unquestioningly, and the man goes along with it because the facsimile is better than nothing.

All goes well until they travel into town. The boy doesn't want to go, and with good reason: shortly after they arrive he disappears, but another family suddenly recovers a daughter believed to be dead. The man guesses the truth—that the Martian is shaped by the desires of others, and by his own need to fulfill them—and goes to fetch Tom back. But the Martian can't change: the wishes of the new family are too strong for him. "'You are Tom, you *were* Tom, weren't you?'" the man asks plaintively. "'I'm not anyone, I'm just myself,'"[28] says the Martian. A curious statement; this equation of selfhood with nonentity.[29] "'Wherever I am, I am something . . .'" says the Martian. And so it proves. The Martian turns back into Tom, but the new family gives chase, and so do all the people the Martian passes as he runs away, with his mirror-like "face like silver" shining in the lights of the town. Cornered, the Martian screams, face after face flitting across his own. "He was melting wax shaping to their minds," says Bradbury, "his face dissolving to each demand." He collapses and dies, a puddle of various features, unrecognizable.

Once I'd begun to publish books, and to see them reviewed— and to find that several people I didn't much recognize were running around out there with my name on them—this story took on a new significance. "So that's it. My face is melting," I thought. "I'm really a Martian." It does explain a lot. Keats praised negative capability,[30] and unless a writer has something of this quality, she will write characters that are mere mouthpieces for her own views. But if she has too much negative capability, doesn't she risk being turned into melting wax by the strength of her audience's desires and fears, interacting with her own? How many writers have put on other faces, or had other faces thrust upon them, and then been unable to get them off?

At the beginning of this chapter I raised three questions. The first was about writers and readers—for whom does the writer write? The answers have included Nobody and the admiring Bog. The second question was about books. Considering the book's position as the intermediate point between writer and reader, what is the book's function, or its duty?

The use of the word "duty" assumes something with a will of its own, and the book as autonomous creature is a literary notion worth examining. There's a department of the post office called the Dead Letter Office, for letters that can't be delivered. This term implies that all the other letters are alive; which is nonsense, of course, but nonetheless an ancient and pervasive way of thinking. For instance, the Bible has often been called the living Word of God. Another *for instance:* it was the fashion a few hundred years ago for male writers to speak of their pregnancy—got with wordchild by the Spirit, or even by the Muse, if you can wind your head around that kind of gender transposition: such writers would then describe the book's gestation and its eventual birth. Of course a book is nothing like a baby really—some of the reasons are scatological—but the convention of the living words has been persistent. Thus Elizabeth Barrett

Browning, among many others: "My letters! All dead paper . . .
mute and white!— / And yet they seem alive and quiver-
ing. . . ."[31]

One of my university professors, who was also a poet, used to say
that there was only one real question to be asked about any
work, and that was—is it alive, or is it dead? I happen to agree,
but in what does this aliveness or deadness consist? The biolog-
ical definition would be that living things grow and change, and
can have offspring, whereas dead things are inert. In what way
can a text grow and change and have offspring? Only through its
interaction with a reader, no matter how far away that reader
may be from the writer in time and in space. "Poems don't
belong to those who write them," says the lowly poem-filching
postman to the poet Pablo Neruda in the film *Il Postino*.[32] "They
belong to those who need them." And so it is.

Everything used by human beings as a symbol has its negative
or demonic version, and the most demonic version of the text
with a life of its own that I can remember comes again from
Kafka. There's a Jewish legend concerning the Golem, an artificial man who could be brought to life by having a scroll with the
name of God inscribed on it placed in his mouth. But the Golem
could get out of control and run amok, and then you were in
trouble.[33] Kafka's story is a sort of Golem story. It's called "In the
Penal Colony," and it revolves around a justice machine used by
the administration to execute prisoners, who have not been
informed beforehand of their crime. To start the machine up, a
text with the sentence written on it—a sentence devised by the
former commander of the colony, who is now dead—is inserted
into the top. The sentence is a sentence in both senses of the
word—it's a grammatical sentence, and it's the sentence
imposed on the man to be executed. The justice machine then
carries out its functions by writing the sentence with an array of
pen-like glass needles, in intricate calligraphy and with many
flourishes, on the actual body of the condemned man. The crim-
inal is supposed to achieve illumination after six hours, when he
comes to understand what is being written on him.
"'Enlightenment dawns on the dullest,'" says the officer who

worships this machine. "'It begins around the eyes. From there it spreads out . . . Nothing further happens, the man simply begins to decipher the script, he purses his lips as if he were listening.'"[34] (This is a novel method of teaching reading, which has yet to be tested by the school system.)

The end of the story comes when the officer, realizing that the old letter of the law is now a dead letter, sacrifices himself to his own machine; but this time it doesn't work properly. Its cogs and wheels break off and roll away, but by now the thing has a life of its own and it just keeps on going, scribbling and jabbing, until the officer is dead.

In this story the writer is inhuman, the page is the reader's body, and the text is indecipherable. Poet Milton Acorn has a line that goes, "as a poem erases and re-writes its poet,"[35] which also makes the text the active partner, but I doubt that Kafka's variation is quite what he meant.

More usually, the living word is presented in a much more positive light. In the theatre—particularly the Elizabethan theatre—there was often a moment at the end of a play at which the text stepped out of its frame, so to speak, and the play appeared for a moment to be no play at all, but alive in the same sense as its audience. One of the actors would advance out front and address the audience directly. "Hello, I'm not really who you thought I was; actually I'm an actor, and this is a wig. Hope you enjoyed the play, imperfect though it was, and if you did, please treat us actors gently and give us some applause," was what these speeches in effect were saying. Or there might be a prologue—again, apart from the main action—in which an actor said a few words about the play, and recommended it to the audience, and then stepped back into his frame again and became part of the *dramatis personae*.

These moments of recommendation, or of revelation and conclusion, were recreated by many writers of novels and longer poems in little vignettes, either as a prologue, or as an *envoi*, a sending off. The ancestry of the form is most obvious when a novelist is pretending that his book is some sort of play: Thackeray, for instance, has a section at the beginning of *Vanity*

Fair called "Before the Curtain," in which he says his book is a
puppet show within Vanity Fair itself—a fair that consists of the
readers, among others—and he, the author, is only the Manager
of the Performance. And at the end of the book he says, "Come,
children, let us shut up the box and the puppets, for our play is
played out." But in many prologues or *envois,* the writer reveals
himself as the creator of the work, and writes what amounts to
a defense of the book's character, like a letter accompanying a
job application or something on a patent-medicine bottle, sup-
posedly from a satisfied client.

Or, at the end of the story, the writer may send off his
book as if waving goodbye to it as it sets out on a journey—
he or she wishes it well, and sees it on its way; and he may
say goodbye also to the reader who has been the silent partner and collaborator thus far on the journey. Prologue and
envoi have a lot to say about the complex but intimate connection between writer and book, and then between book
and reader. Quite frequently the book is little—"Go, little
book"—almost as if it is a child, who must now make its own
way in the world; but its way—its duty—consists in carrying
itself to the reader, and delivering itself as best it can. "You
understand," says Primo Levi in a letter to his German trans-
lator, "it is the only book I have written and now . . . I feel
like a father whose son has reached the age of consent and
leaves, and one can no longer look after him."[36] One of the
most disarming *envois* is by François Villon, the rascally and
perennially broke fifteenth-century French poet, who
instructed his poem to get a very urgent message through to
a wealthy prince:

> Go my letter, make a dash
> Though you haven't feet or tongue
> Explain in your harangue
> I'm crushed by lack of cash.[37]

Other writers are less blunt; instead, they display a friendly
concern for the reader. Here is the Russian poet Pushkin, saying a charming goodbye to the reader at the end of his poem,
Eugene Onegin:

Reader, I wish that, as we parted—
whoever you may be, a friend,
a foe—our mood should be warm-hearted.
Goodbye, for now we make an end.
Whatever in this rough confection
you sought—tumultuous recollection,
a rest from all its toils and aches,
or just grammatical mistakes,
a vivid brush, a witty rattle—
God grant that from this little book
for heart's delight, or fun, you took—
for dreams, or journalistic battle,
God grant you took at least a grain.
On this we'll part; goodbye, again.[38]

Two of the earliest and also the most complete pieces of writing of this sort are by John Bunyan; they come at the front of Parts One and Two of *The Pilgrim's Progress*. The Part One prologue, "The Author's Apology for his Book," is more like an advertisement than anything else—these are the many good things this book can do for you, plus a list of the wholesome ingredients—but in the Part Two prologue, called "The Author's Way of Sending Forth his Second Part of the 'Pilgrim,'" the book has become a person:

Go, now my little Book to every place,
Where my first *Pilgrim* has but shown his Face,
Call at their door if any say, "Who's there?"
Then answer thou, "Christiana is here."[39]

Bunyan then gives his book a list of detailed instructions; but the book becomes frightened of its assignment, and begins to answer back. Bunyan reassures it, and replies to its objections by telling it what to say in various difficult situations; and finally he tells it, or her, that no matter how wonderful she is, there will be some people that won't like her, because that's just the way it is:

Some love no Cheese, some love no Fish, and some
Love not their Friends, nor their own house or home;
Some start at Pig, slight Chicken, love not Fowl,
More than they love a Cuckoo or an Owl.
Leave such, my Christiana, to their choice,
And seek those who to find thee will rejoice . . .[40]

Useful and bracing advice for any book, I think. The Ancient Mariner has an auditor who cannot choose but hear, but not all narrators have such a glittering eye, or such luck. Bunyan concludes with a very Protestant, fiscally honest, frugal, cheap-for-the-price sort of prayer:

> Now may this little Book a blessing be,
> To those that love this little Book and me,
> And may its Buyer have no cause to say,
> His Money is but lost or thrown away . . .[41]

Christiana has turned back into a book, a book-as-object, and an object that is for sale.

Such transformations—from book to person, from person to book—are in fact quite common. They can also be quite double-edged. We all know that a book is not really a person. It isn't a human being. But if you are a lover of books as books—as objects, that is—and ignore the human element in them—that is, their voices—you will be committing an error of the soul, because you will be an idolator, or else a fetishist. This is the fate of Peter Kien, the protagonist of Elias Canetti's novel *Auto da Fé*. *Auto da fé* means "act of faith," and refers to the mass burnings of "heretics" once put on by the Inquisition. Kien is a collector of books, and loves their physical presence, though he detests novels—they have too much feeling in them. He loves these book-objects of his, but in a twisted way: he hoards them; and we know he's in spiritual trouble when he refuses to let a little boy who is hungry for knowledge read any of them, and instead kicks him downstairs.

Early in the book, Kien has a nightmare. The scene is a bonfire, combined with an Aztec-style human sacrifice, but when the victim's chest is cut open, instead of a heart, out comes a book—and then another book, and then another. These books fall into the flames. Kien tells the victim to close up his chest, to save the books, but no: more and more books pour out. Kien rushes into the fire to save them, but whenever he puts out his hand to save a book, he clutches a shrieking human being. "'Let me go,'" Kien shouts. "'I don't know you. What do you want with me! How can I rescue the books!'"[42]

But he's missed the point. The human beings in the dream *are* the books—they are the human element in the books. He hears the voice of God, which says, "'There are no books here,'" but he misinterprets it. At the end of the novel, all the books he has collected come to life and turn against him—they are his prisoners, he has locked them up in his private library, and now they want their messages set free; for, as I've said, books must travel from reader to reader in order to stay alive. Finally he sets fire to them, and himself along with them: an *auto da fé*, the fate of a heretic. As the books burn, he can hear their letters escaping from the Dead Letter Office he has created, out into the world again.

Sometimes the book is allowed to speak on its own behalf, without the writer's intervention. Here is a poem by Jay Macpherson, called simply "Book." Not only is this a talking book, it's a riddle, the answer to which is contained in its title.

> Dear Reader, not your fellow flesh and blood
> —I cannot love like you, nor you like me—
> But like yourself launched out upon the flood,
> Poor vessel to endure so fierce a sea.
>
> The water-beetle travelling dry and frail
> On the stream's face is not more slight than I;
> Nor more tremendous is the ancient whale
> Who scans the ocean floor with horny eye.
>
> Although by my creator's will I span
> The air, the fire, the water and the land,
> My volume is no burden to your hand.
>
> I flourish in your sight and for your sake.
> His servant, yet I grapple fast with man:
> Grasped and devoured, I bless him. Reader, take.[43]

As well as being a boat, a whale, and the angel who wrestled with Jacob and blessed him, the little book is the object of consumption in a communion meal—the food that may be devoured but never destroyed, the feast that renews itself as well as the feast-guests' link with the spiritual. The angel must not only be grappled with, it must be assimilated by the reader, so that it becomes a part of him or her.[44] This brings me to my last question: where is the writer when the reader is reading? There are two answers to that. First, the writer is nowhere. In his small piece called "Borges and I," Jorge Luis Borges inserts a parenthetical aside about his own existence. "(If it is true that I am someone)" he says.[45] By the time we, the readers, come to read those lines, that's a very big *if*, because by the time the reader is reading, the writer may not even exist. The writer is thus the original invisible man: not there at all but also very solidly there, at one and the same time, because the second answer to the question—*Where is the writer when the reader is reading?*—is, "Right here." At least we have the impression that he or she is right here, in the same room with us—we can hear the voice. Or we can almost hear the voice. Or we can hear *a* voice. Or so it seems. As the Russian writer Abram Tertz says in his story "The Icicle," "Look, I'm smiling at you, I'm smiling in you, I'm smiling through you. How can I be dead if I breathe in every quiver of your hand?"[46]

In Carol Shields's novel *Swann: A Mystery*,[47] about a murdered woman poet and also about her readers, we find out that the original versions of the dead woman's poems are no longer fully legible—they were written on scraps of old envelopes and got thrown into the garbage by mistake, which blurred them quite a bit. Not only that, a resentful connoisseur has gone around destroying the few remaining copies of the first edition. But several readers have luckily memorized the poems, or parts of them, and at the end of the book they create—or recreate— one of these poems before our very eyes, by reciting the fragments. "Isis keeps Osiris alive by remembering him," says Dudley Young.[48] "Remembering" as a pun may of course have two senses—it is the act of memory, but it is also the opposite of dismembering. Or this is what the ear hears. Any reader creates by assembling the fragments of a read book—we can read, after all, only in fragments—and making them into an organic whole in her mind.

Perhaps you will remember the end of Ray Bradbury's futuristic nightmare, *Fahrenheit 451*.[49] All the books are being burnt, in favor of wraparound TV screens that allow for more complete social control. Our hero, who begins as a fireman helping to destroy the books,[50] becomes a convert to the secret resistance movement dedicated to preserving books and, along with them, human history and thought. At length he finds himself in a forest where the insurgents are hiding out. Each has *become* a book, by memorizing it. The fireman is introduced to Socrates, Jane Austen, Charles Dickens, and many more, all of them reciting the books they have assimilated, or "devoured." The reader has in effect eliminated the middle point of the triangle—the text in its paper version—and has actually become the book, or vice versa.

With this circuit complete, I will go back to the first question—for whom does the writer write? And I will give two answers. The first is a story about my first real reader.

When I was nine, I was enrolled in a secret society, complete with special handshakes, slogans, rituals, and mottoes. The name of this was the Brownies, and it was quite bizarre. The little girls in it pretended to be fairies, gnomes, and elves, and the grownup leading it was called Brown Owl. Sadly, she did not wear an owl costume, nor did the little girls wear fairy outfits. This was a disappointment to me, but not a fatal one.

I did not know the real name of Brown Owl, but I thought she was wise and fair, and as I needed someone like that in my life at the time, I adored this Brown Owl. Part of the program involved completing various tasks, for which you might collect badges to sew on to your uniform, and in aid of various badge-collecting projects—needlework stitches, seeds of autumn, and so forth—I made some little books, in the usual way: I folded the pages, and sewed them together with sock-darning wool. I then inserted text and illustrations. I gave these books to Brown Owl, and the fact that she liked them was certainly more important to me than the badges. This was my first real writer-reader relationship. The writer, me; the go-between, my books; the recipient, Brown Owl; the result, pleasure for her, and gratification for me.

Many years later, I put Brown Owl into a book. There she is, still blowing her whistle and supervising the knot tests, in my novel *Cat's Eye,* for the same reason that a lot of things and people are put into books. That was in the 1980s, and I was sure the original Brown Owl must have been long dead by then.

Then a few years ago a friend said to me, "Your Brown Owl is my aunt." "Is?" I said. "She can't possibly be alive!" But she was, so off we went to visit her. She was well over ninety, but Brown Owl and I were very pleased to see each other. After we'd had tea, she said, "I think you should have these," and she took out the little books I had made fifty years before—which for some reason she'd kept—and gave them back to me. She died three days later.

That's my first answer: the writer writes for Brown Owl, or for whoever the equivalent of Brown Owl may be in his or her life at the time. A real person, then: singular, specific.

Here's my second answer. At the end of Isak Dinesen's "The Young Man With the Carnation," God's voice makes itself heard to the young writer Charlie, who has been so despairing about his work. "'Come,' said the Lord. 'I will make a covenant between Me and you. I, I will not measure you out any more distress than you need to write your books . . . But you are to write the books. For it is I who want them written. Not the public, not by any means the critics, but Me, Me!' 'Can I be certain of that?' asked Charlie. 'Not always!' said the Lord."[51]

So that is who the writer writes for: for the reader. For the reader who is not Them, but You. For the Dear Reader. For the ideal reader, who exists on a continuum somewhere between Brown Owl and God. And this ideal reader may prove to be anyone at all—any *one* at all—because the act of reading is just as singular—always—as the act of writing.

(2002)

ENDNOTES

1. Henry Fielding, *Tom Jones* (New York: Signet, Penguin, 1963, 1979), pp. 24–5.
2. Walter Benjamin, "The Storyteller," Hannah Arendt (ed.), *Illuminations* (New York: Schocken Books, 1969), p. 100.
3. Peter Gay, *The Pleasure Wars* (New York: Norton, 1998), p. 39.

4. Gwendolyn MacEwen, "The Choice," *The Rising Fire* (Toronto: Contact Éditions, 1963), p. 71.
5. Henry James, "The Death of the Lion," *The Lesson of the Master and Other Stories* (London: John Lehmann, 1948), p. 86.
6. Anne Michaels, "Letters from Martha," *Miner's Pond, The Weight of Oranges, Skin Divers* (London: Bloomsbury, 2000), pp. 32–3.
7. John Le Carré, *Smiley's People* (New York: Bantam, 1974).
8. What he actually said was, "The poet is not heard, he is overheard." Northrop Frye said this frequently in lectures attended by the author during her undergraduate studies at the University of Toronto.
9. Hjalmar Söderberg, Paul Britten Austin (trans.), *Doctor Glas* (first published 1905) (London: Tandem, 1963), p. 16.
10. George Orwell, *Nineteen Eighty-Four* (Harmondsworth, Middlesex: Penguin, 1949), pp. 8–9.
11. Ibid., p. 10.
12. Emily Dickinson, "441 [This is my letter to the World,]" Thomas H. Johnson (ed.), *The Complete Poems of Emily Dickinson* (Boston: Little, Brown, 1890, 1960), p. 211.
13. Stephen King, *Misery* (New York: Viking, Penguin, 1987).
14. Gaston Leroux, *The Phantom of the Opera* (New York: HarperCollins, 1988).
15. Edmond Rostand, *Cyrano de Bergerac* (first published 1897) (New York: Bantam, 1954).
16. Dedicatee of *Shakespeare's Sonnets.*
17. Dickinson, "288 [I'm Nobody! Who are you?]," *Complete Poems,* p. 133.
18. "Hypocrite reader!—You!—My twin!—My brother!" Charles Baudelaire, "To the Reader," Roy Campbell (trans.), *Flowers of Evil* (Norfolk, USA: New Directions, 1955), p. 4.
19. Marilyn Monroe, as mentioned in various biographical pieces.
20. John Keats, Letter to Benjamin Robert Haydon, May 10–11, 1817, Douglas Bush (ed.), *Selected Poems and Letters* (Cambridge, MA: Riverside Press, 1959).
21. Graham Greene, *The End of the Affair* (New York: Penguin, 1999), p. 129.
22. Ibid., p. 148.
23. Cyril Connolly, *Enemies of Promise* (Harmondsworth, Middlesex: Penguin, 1961), p. 129.
24. Ibid., p. 134.
25. Ibid., p. 133.
26. Ibid.
27. Isak Dinesen, "The Young Man With the Carnation," *Winter's Tales* (New York: Vintage, 1993), p. 4.

28. Ray Bradbury, "The Martian," *The Martian Chronicles* (New York: Bantam, 1946, 1977), p. 127.
29. It is worth noting in relation to chapter 2 that Borges was a fan of *The Martian Chronicles*. See Jorge Luis Borges, "Ray Bradbury: The Martian Chronicles," Eliot Weinberger (ed., trans.), *The Total Library: Non-Fiction 1922–1986* (London: Allen Lane, Penguin Press, 1999), pp. 418–19.
30. Keats defined negative capability as: ". . . when man is capable of being in uncertainties, mysteries, doubts, without any irritable reaching after fact and reason." Letter to George and Thomas Keats, December 22, 1817, *Selected Poems and Letters*.
31. Elizabeth Barrett Browning, "Sonnets from the Portuguese," xxviii, E. K. Brown and J. O. Bailey (eds.), *Victorian Poetry* (New York: Ronald Press, 1962).
32. *Il Postino,* written by Massimo Troisi et al., directed by Michael Radford.
33. Eduard Petiska and Jana Svábová (trans.), *Golem* (Prague: Martin, 1991).
34. Franz Kafka, "In the Penal Colony," *The Transformation and Other Stories* (London: Penguin, 1992), p. 137.
35. Milton Acorn, "Knowing I Live in a Dark Age," Margaret Atwood (ed.), *The New Oxford Book of Canadian Verse in English* (Toronto: Oxford University Press Canada, 1982), p. 238.
36. Primo Levi, Raymond Rosenthal (trans.), *The Drowned and the Saved* (London: Abacus, 1999), p. 142.
37. François Villon, "Ballade [My lord and fearsome prince]," Galway Kinnell (ed.), *The Poems of François Villon* (Boston: Houghton Mifflin, 1977), p. 197.
38. Alexander Pushkin, "Eugene Onegin," Avraham Yarmolinsky (ed.), *The Poems, Prose and Plays of Alexander Pushkin* (New York: The Modern Library, 1936), p. 301.
39. John Bunyan, Roger Sharrock (ed.), *The Pilgrim's Progress* (London: Penguin, 1987), p. 147.
40. Ibid., pp. 151–2.
41. Ibid., p. 153.
42. Elias Canetti, *Auto da Fé* (New York: Picador, Pan Books, 1978), p. 35.
43. Jay Macpherson, "Book," Robert Weaver and William Toye (eds.), *The Oxford Anthology of Canadian Literature* (Toronto: Oxford University Press Canada, 1973), p. 322.
44. The word as food is an ancient concept. Christ in the New Testament is the Word made Flesh, and the flesh is the flesh of the Communion meal. See also the edible scroll (Isaiah 34:4) and the edible book (Revelation 10: 8–10). And for sheer pleasure, see the

Prologue to *Tom Jones,* in which Fielding presents a Bill of Fare
for his book, which he likens to a meal at an inn. Henry Fielding,
Tom Jones (New York: Signet, Penguin, 1963, 1979).
45. Jorge Luis Borges, "Borges and I," James E. Irby (trans.), *Every-thing and Nothing* (New York: New Directions, 1999), p. 74.
46. Abram Tertz, "The Icicle," *The Icicle and Other Stories* (London: Collins and Harvill, 1963).
47. Carol Shields, *Swann: A Mystery* (Toronto: Stoddart, 1987).
48. Dudley Young, *Origins of the Sacred: The Ecstasies of Love and War* (New York: St. Martin's Press, 1991), p. 325.
49. Ray Bradbury, *Fahrenheit 451* (New York: Ballantine Books, 1995).
50. Compare the memory-hole in Orwell, *Nineteen Eighty-Four,* and the book destruction in Bohumile Hrabal, Michael Henry Heim (trans.), *Too Loud a Solitude* (London: Abacus, 1990) or in Ursula K. LeGuin, *The Telling* (New York: Harcourt, 2000).
51. Dinesen, "The Young Man With the Carnation," p. 25. Many writ-ers have of course felt they wrote by order of God, or some god—the one that has most recently come to my attention is Canadian novelist Margaret Laurence, who confessed this to fellow writer Matt Cohen. See *Typing* (Toronto: Knopf Canada, 2000), p. 186.